DEVELOPMENT AND UNDERDEVELOPMENT

Series editors: Ray Bromley and Gavin Kitching

Development Projects as Policy Experiments

AN ADAPTIVE APPROACH TO DEVELOPMENT ADMINISTRATION

In the same series

Already published:

Development and Underdevelopment in Historical Perspective: Populism, nationalism and industrialization
Gavin Kitching

Forthcoming:

Class Conflict and the Rural Environment in Developing Countries
Michael Redclift

Development Strategies and Debates in Communist States
Robert Bideleux

Latin American Development Theories: Structuralism, internal colonialism, marginality and dependency
Cristóbal Kay

Marketplace and Marketing System: A developmental perspective
Ray Bromley

Multinational Corporations
Rhys Jenkins

Regions in Question: Space and regional planning in development
Charles Gore

Unequal Exchange and the World Division of Labour
Chris Edwards

Latin American Theories of Development and Underdevelopment
Cristóbal Kay

Development Projects as Policy Experiments

AN ADAPTIVE APPROACH
TO DEVELOPMENT ADMINISTRATION

Dennis A. Rondinelli

ROUTLEDGE
London & New York

First published in 1983 by
Methuen & Co. Ltd

Reprinted by Routledge 1990
11 New Fetter Lane, London EC4P 4EE

Simultaneously published in the USA and Canada
by Routledge
a division of Routledge, Chapman and Hall, Inc.
29 West 35th Street, New York, NY 10001

British Library Cataloguing in Publication Data
Rondinelli, Dennis A.
    Development projects as policy experiments.—
    (Development and underdevelopment)
    1. Economic development projects—Underdeveloped
    areas—Management
    I. Title.   II. Series
    658.4′04   HD69.P75

    ISBN 0–415–00370–9

Library of Congress Cataloging in Publication Data
Rondinelli, Dennis A.
    Development projects as policy experiments.

    (Development and underdevelopment)
    Bibliography: p.
    Includes index.
    1. Economic development projects—management.
    I. Title.   II. Series.
    HD82.R675   1983   338.9′00968   83–8117
    ISBN 0–415–00370–9

Contents

SERIES EDITORS' PREFACE   vii

PREFACE   viii

1 The problem of development administration:
  coping with complexity and uncertainty   1

2 Development policies as social experiments   23

3 Designing development projects: the limits
  of comprehensive planning and management   65

4 Implementing development projects as policy
  experiments: toward adaptive administration   89

5 Reorienting development administration:
  principles, problems and opportunities   116

BIBLIOGRAPHY   149

INDEX   163

Series editors' preface

Development studies is a complex and diverse field of academic research and policy analysis. Concerned with the development process in all the comparatively poor nations of the world, it covers an enormous geographical area and a large part of the modern history of the world. Such a large subject area has generated a varied body of literature in a growing number of journals and other specialist publications, encompassing such diverse issues as the nature and feasibility of industrialization, the problem of small-scale agriculture and rural development in the Third World, the trade and other links between developed and developing countries and their effects on the development prospects of the poor, the nature and causes of poverty and inequality, and the record and future prospects of 'development planning' as a method of accelerating development. The nature of the subject matter has forced both scholars and practitioners to transcend the boundaries of their own disciplines whether these be social sciences, like economics, human geography or sociology, or applied sciences such as agronomy, plant biology or civil engineering. It is now a conventional wisdom of development studies that development problems are so multi-faceted and complex that *no* single discipline can hope to encompass them, let alone offer solutions.

This large and interdisciplinary area and the complex and rapidly changing literature pose particular problems for students, practitioners and specialists seeking a simple introduction to the field or some part of the field with which they are unfamiliar. The Development and Underdevelopment series attempts to rectify these problems by providing a number of brief, readable introductions to important issues in development studies written by an international range of specialists. All the texts are designed to be readily comprehensible to students meeting the issues for the first time, as well as to practitioners in developing countries, international agencies and voluntary bodies. We hope that, taken together, these books will bring to the reader a sense of the main preoccupations and problems in this rich and stimulating field of study and practice. RAY BROMLEY
GAVIN KITCHING

Preface

As the development strategies of international assistance agencies and poor countries became more complex over the past few decades, methods of planning and managing development policies, programs and projects became less effective. The comprehensive planning and systems management techniques used during the 1960s and 1970s were aimed at controlling development activities and are incapable of coping with the complexity and uncertainty of emerging problems. They do not encourage the flexibility, experimentation and social learning that are crucial to implementing complex and uncertain ventures successfully.

Conventional planning and administrative methods have resulted in costly but ineffective analysis, greater inconsistency and uncertainty, the delegation of important development activities to technical experts, inappropriate and sometimes harmful intervention, the failure to include beneficiaries in decision-making, and reluctance on the part of administrators to detect and correct errors. The prospects of improving control-oriented management are constrained by the difficulties of defining objectives concisely, lack of appropriate data, inadequate understanding of local social and cultural conditions, ineffective means of controlling behavior, the dynamics of political interaction, and low levels of administrative capacity in developing countries.

Development administration must be reoriented to cope more effectively with the inevitable uncertainty and complexity of development problems in the coming decades. One of the most promising ways is to use an adaptive approach that relies on adjunctive and strategic planning, on administrative procedures that facilitate innovation, responsiveness and experimentation, and on decision-making processes that join learning with action.

It is appropriate that a book which recommends a learning-based approach to planning and administration is the result of my own learning experience over more than a decade and a half. The ideas presented here are the result of an incremental, experimental and experiential learning process; I have formulated, revised and reformulated them a number of times in articles during the past ten years and tested them in development projects for which I have served as an advisor in one capacity or another. This book not only brings them together but also presents them in a substantially revised, expanded and reorganized form. As is the case with any ideas that are the result of learning and experimentation, I expect that they will change as I and others continue to test them in the future. Thus, I see them as propositions about the nature of development problems and policies that can provide guides to action, but that are still evolving and need continuous testing and verification in new and changing circumstances.

Discussions with many people involved directly in development policy-making and implementation helped shape the ideas in this book. The bibliography indicates more specifically those from whose experience and thinking I have learned the most. I am especially grateful to Ray Bromley, Marcus Ingle, David Korten and Edward Rizzo, who read and reacted to various sections of this book in their present or previous forms. I retain full responsibility, of course, for the conclusions and interpretations.

DENNIS A. RONDINELLI
Syracuse, New York

1

The problem of development administration: coping with complexity and uncertainty

Experience with development during the past quarter century has led to two fundamental discoveries. First, it became clear that many of the conventional theories of economic growth that had been applied in developing nations during the 1950s and 1960s did not achieve their intended goals. Despite the relatively high levels of growth in gross national product, disparities in living conditions between rich and poor nations and between the highest and lowest income groups within Third World countries continued to widen. The trickle down and spread effects that had been expected to follow increases in industrial output either did not occur or did little to alleviate widespread poverty. Thus, they did not establish a base for sustained economic growth. New and more complex strategies emerged during the 1970s to reduce the dependence of poor countries on the industrialized economies, spread the benefits of development to lagging regions within developing countries, and increase the productivity and income of the poorest groups. Second, it became clear that as strategies became more complex, the success of development programs and projects became less certain. Methods of planning and management associated with earlier strategies were found to be less useful in coping with the uncertainty and complexity of development problems.

The experience of the past quarter century indicates that rapidly changing and disparate theories of economic development have been, and will continue to be, uncertain propositions that are shaped by complex processes of political interaction and social learning. But the administrative procedures that are used by international organizations and the governments of developing countries to apply development theories have never adequately reflected these underlying uncertainties. Nor have those who have applied them recognized explicitly that all development policies are really social experiments. Governments and international organizations still attempt to use planning and management techniques to *control* development activities rather than to facilitate and encourage the flexibility, experimentation, and social learning that are essential to implementing development projects successfully. Administrators have yet to come to grips with the experimental nature of development policies and with the uncertainties inherent in their implementation.

This book explores the growing divergence between the nature of development problems and the principles of development administration, at least as they have been defined by international assistance agencies and the governments of many developing countries over the past two decades. It examines a major dilemma of development administration: planners and policy-makers who work in bureaucracies that seek to control rather than to facilitate development activities must cope with the increasing uncertainty and complexity of development problems, but the controls inhibit the kinds of analysis and planning that are most appropriate to dealing with them.

THE GAP BETWEEN THEORY AND REALITY

Although the rhetoric of development policy has changed drastically over the past quarter of a century, perspectives on the nature of development planning and administration have changed very little. In the 1950s and 1960s development planners prescribed long-range, comprehensive, national planning and centrally controlled, "top-down" systems of decision-making to formulate and implement development policies. During the 1970s most international development organizations and governments in developing countries adopted what Lindblom (1965) calls a "synoptic" approach to decision-making. As he points out, those who hold a rationalistic view of decision-making believe that complex social problems can be understood through systematic analysis and solved through comprehensive planning. They assume the existence of authoritative and objective decision-makers whose actions can, if they are carried out correctly, ameliorate economic and social adversities. They believe that exhaustive analysis will lead to a concise definition of problems, and generate alternatives from which optimal and correct policy choices can be made. They further believe that models or theories of social change can be constructed to aid in problem definition and policy formulation, that those policies will respond adequately to human needs and that there is a direct relationship between government action and the solution of social problems (Braybrooke and Lindblom, 1970).

Because the policies emanate from rational and comprehensive analysis, plans must be carried out through a hierarchical structure of authority, which imposes rules and regulations. Deviations from preconceived plans are considered detrimental to achieving what are assumed to be commonly held objectives. Conflicts over goals, values or courses of action are seen, therefore, as adverse and irrational manifestations of politics and the pursuit of selfish interests. Thus, political conflict is to be avoided. Planners and policy-makers are to determine the correct courses of action for others to follow and to establish rules and procedures that ensure adherence to them.

Although some officials of international funding organizations would not espouse this explicit interpretation of their views, a highly rationalistic approach was reflected in the methods of planning and management that they adopted during the 1970s. Officials of the World Bank, most bilateral aid institutions and many United Nations agencies insisted that development projects be identified, prepared, appraised, and selected through comprehensive and systematic analysis. They used methods and procedures adopted largely from the practices of private corporations engaged in physical construction projects and of government agencies in Western countries concerned with defense systems or space exploration. The methods included cost-benefit analysis, linear programming models, network scheduling, and planning-programming-budgeting systems. Since international lending institutions provided much of the funding for development projects their procedures and controls, which they considered to be modern management systems, could be easily transferred to bureaucracies in many developing states. Paradoxically, as development strategies changed during the 1970s to address more complicated and less controllable problems of human development, procedures for planning and managing projects became more rigid and routinized (Rondinelli, 1976; 1979).

Rarely, however, have development policies been carried out in the prescribed ways, and this disparity between theory and reality is at the heart of recurrent debates over the effectiveness of development planning and administration (Rondinelli, 1977; 1978; 1979). Although this book is concerned primarily with policy-making processes, it focuses particularly on projects as instruments of policy implementation to examine this disparity. The emphasis is placed on projects for a number of reasons. Most obviously, they have become the primary means through which governments of developing countries attempt to translate their plans and policies into programs of action. No matter how comprehensive and detailed developments plans seem to be, they are of little value unless they can be translated into projects or programs that can be carried out. Thus, projects have become important channels through which governments and international assistance organizations invest their resources.

For this reason, projects have come to play a central role in the political economy of developing countries. Hirschman (1967: 1) has called them "privileged particles of the development process," and Gittinger (1972: 1) sees them at the "cutting edge" of development administration. Projects can influence the processes through which economic changes occur by integrating markets, linking productive activities in the public and private sectors, providing the organization and technology for transforming raw materials into economically and socially useful products, and creating the physical infrastructure needed to increase exchange and trade (Uphoff and Ilchman, 1972). In many countries projects also stimulate social change: education, health, family planning and social services projects help to satisfy basic human needs and provide new skills required in traditional societies to initiate and sustain modernization.

Successful projects can generate new resources for further investment, creating a momentum for continued and widespread economic progress. In this sense, Hirschman (1967: 1) is correct in calling development projects a special kind of investment: "the term connotes purposefulness, some minimum size, a specific location, the introduction of something qualitatively new, and the expectation that a sequence of further development moves will be set in motion." Because they are considered by their sponsors to be manageable sets of activities, projects are likely to remain the primary means of translating development policies and aid strategies into programs of action.

A substantial amount of evidence also suggests that translating plans into projects is one of the most difficult tasks facing development administrators. For more than two decades analysts have pointed out that there has been "a scarcity of well prepared projects ready to go and . . . the lack of projects reduces the number of productive investment opportunities" (Waterston, 1971: 240). The United Nations Economic Commission for Africa (1969: 137) has noted that "in many countries essential pieces of development cannot be carried out at the time when they are required, not solely because of financial shortages, but because the projects themselves have not been technically prepared," and other UN agencies have noted (1969: 69) that "there are many cases where the shortage of good projects is even more serious than the shortage of capital or foreign exchange."

Finally, the focus on projects affords the best opportunity to illustrate the disjunction between methods of planning and implementation used by governments and international agencies and the nature of development problems. Experience thus far with growth-with-equity and basic-human-needs approaches strongly indicates that they are not amenable to systematic analysis or to comprehensive design. The increasing concern in developing nations with alleviating poverty, increasing agricultural productivity, expanding employment opportunities and providing greater access to social services for larger numbers of people has made project design more complex and the success of projects more uncertain. As will be seen in chapter 3, many problems have arisen during implementation from attempts to plan and manage projects aimed at generating social change with techniques and procedures intended for physical facilities and industrial construction projects. Evaluations are beginning to indicate, as did a review of small-scale agricultural projects in Africa and Latin America, that flexibility in planning and design, opportunity to adjust plans as projects progress, and continuous redesign during implementation, are essential for success. "Few projects can survive a rigid blueprint which fixes at the time of implementation the development approaches, priorities, and mechanisms for achieving success," the evaluators (Morss et al., 1975: 329) noted. "Most projects scoring high on success experienced at least one major revision after the project [managers] determined that the original plan was not working." A large degree of flexibility is critical, they argued, "particularly if the technology is uncertain or if the local constraints facing small farmers are not well known." The argument for greater flexibility and innovativeness in project planning and management rests in part on the observation that development policies are complex and uncertain. The drastic changes that have occurred in development theories and strategies over the past quarter of a century require flexible and experimental methods of implementation.

THE TREND TOWARD TECHNOCRACY

The methods of planning, analysis and management introduced during the 1960s and 1970s, and which still dominate the procedures of most international organizations and governments in developing countries, however, were not primarily concerned with flexibility, responsiveness and learning. They were more concerned with efficiency and control. Systems approaches were introduced not only because they were compatible with macro-economic concepts of development prevalent during the 1950s and 1960s, but also because they were perceived as effective methods of reducing uncertainty and increasing the influence of technocrats. Ironically, politicians and administrators embraced control-oriented planning and management techniques that were either ineffective or inherently incapable of reducing uncertainty at a time when the recognition that development was an uncertain process was becoming widespread.

The principles underlying systems approaches to planning and management were compatible with the growth maximization strategies prescribed by macro-economists during the 1950s and 1960s. Their adoption, as Benveniste (1972: 27) points out, was also quite consistent with the "conventional notion that planners and government need strong power to plan; that planning has to be 'imperative' in nature; and that short of centralization and strong executive control to impose the plan, it will fail." It was reinforced by the growing realization that despite the preparation of national development plans governments in developing countries controlled few of the major factors affecting economic and social change. In many cases rationalistic and synoptic approaches to planning and management were related "to the inability of organizations or entire governments to function in an environment that has become too uncertain" (Benveniste, 1972: 24). Moreover, the trend toward quantification and the introduction of technocratic methods of analysis and management wrapped national planners and foreign experts in the mantle of authoritativeness. Their tools became their power. As Benveniste (p. 57) notes, "the expert's dependency on measurement is very real. Measurements and quantitative analysis are the bases of the knowledge which differentiates them and, therefore, a basis of their social power. They cannot spend too much time talking in vague ways. Sooner or later they need to concentrate on the issues on which they can exercise their skills."

In addition, the adoption of rational, synoptic and quantitative methods of planning suited the needs of politicians in many developing countries, for such methods offered a variety of benefits that were not directly related to their ostensible function of selecting economically feasible and optimal courses of action (Benveniste, 1972; Davis, 1974; Rondinelli, 1975). Systematic analysis and synoptic planning can be used to legitimize decisions that have already been made or to justify not taking any action to resolve pressing political issues. They can be used to raise the priority of some political options that are not popular and to remove others from the policy agenda. They are a means of making fundamentally political decisions seem objective and technical and of altering the time horizon for decision-making from the present to the future. Often the mere attempt to do such analysis and planning is a symbol of rationality and objectivity. Central planning and control is a means of constraining the process of political interaction and of limiting the influence and discretion of the bureaucracy and other potential interest groups. Finally, the procedures often serve as "window-dressing" to meet the requirements of international agencies and national finance and planning ministries for systematic analysis and planning.

CHANGING PERCEPTIONS OF OPTIMUM DEVELOPMENT STRATEGIES

The directions of international development policy shifted drastically in the early 1970s from a predominant concern with promoting rapid growth in gross national product through capital-intensive industrialization, export production and construction of large-scale physical infrastructure to ways of stimulating internal demand, expanding economic participation, developing human resources and reducing disparities in income and wealth. The new policies were less concerned with the rate of aggregate economic growth than with its composition and the distribution of its benefits.

Changes in development policies during the 1970s resulted from a number of converging forces. In part, they evolved from the realization that post-World War II macro-economic development strategies had not been effective. The trickle down and spread effects promised by conventional economic theory had not materialized in much of the developing world and could no longer be used as the basis for planning. Nearly half of the 187 nations surveyed by the World Bank in 1974 had a per capita GNP below $500 a year, and only nineteen reported levels above $5000. The majority of countries with a per capita GNP below $300 during the 1960s also had an annual growth rate of less than 5 percent. About thirty desperately poor countries with intransigent social and economic problems, and with a substantial portion of the world's population, had been by-passed entirely by economic progress. Moreover, the distribution of income and wealth, even within growing economies, remained highly inequitable. The World Bank estimated in the mid-1970s that nearly 85 percent, or more than 750 million, of the people in developing nations were living in relative poverty, earning less than $75 a year; two-fifths subsisted in absolute poverty on annual incomes of less than $50 (World Bank, 1975).

New strategies also emerged from internal social and political pressures: from widespread recognition of the social injustices perpetuated by dual economies and from the realization by national leaders that political stability and national unity could not be achieved or maintained only with narrow support from a small, wealthy, urban elite. Moreover, the success of experiments with more equitable growth policies in some communist and socialist societies created pressures on governments with mixed economies to reduce the growing gaps in income and wealth.

International evaluation commissions frequently criticized development policies and aid strategies as inadequate or inappropriate. The Pearson Commission (1969) noted that growth in the economies of many poor nations continued to be outpaced by population increases, thereby "nullifying much of the development effort." Seemingly successful development policies simply produced new and more difficult problems. As massive educational development programs began to reduce illiteracy and ignorance, frustrations were created for millions of young graduates who could not find jobs in stagnant economies. As crop yields and food supplies were increased by the success of agricultural development programs, new problems of production, distribution and marketing emerged with which governments in many developing countries had neither the resources nor the technical capabilities to cope. Even modest economic progress generated new expectations that governments could not fulfill. "In supplying such facilities as schools, hospitals and urban housing," the Pearson Commission (1969: 12–13) reported, "even a holding operation to keep standards from slipping is often difficult."

When it became clear in the late 1960s that capital-intensive industrialization policies had been ineffective in promoting growth and alleviating poverty in most developing countries, new strategies and goals appeared in national development plans. India's plan for the 1970s admitted explicitly that the benefits of aggregate economic growth had not filtered down to the vast majority of the people and that without more widespread participation in economic activities growth could not be accelerated or sustained. "Growthmanship which results in undivided attention to the maximization of GNP can be dangerous," Indian analysts noted. "Elimination of abject poverty will not be attained as a corollary to a certain acceleration of the growth of the economy alone" (Das, 1973: 430). Similar conclusions were expressed in the policy pronouncements of other countries. In its 1974–78 national plan the Philippine government proclaimed "that no longer is maximum economic growth at the singular apex of goals; equally desirable are maximum employment, promotion of social development and more equitable distribution of income and wealth." Thailand's plans for the 1970s sought to balance national development more equally among its geographical regions and restructure the economy to reduce income inequalities, develop human resources and expand rural employment. Development plans in many African and Middle Eastern countries began to stress the importance of employment generation and wider distribution of income (Nigam, 1975).

Bilateral and international assistance organizations also modified their aid strategies in the early 1970s. The United States Congress issued a new mandate to the US Agency for International Development (USAID) in 1973, for instance, to give the highest priority to activities in developing nations that "directly improve the lives of the poorest of their people and their capacity to participate in the development of their countries." In the Foreign Assistance Act of 1973, Congress declared that the conditions under which American foreign aid had been provided in the past had changed, and that policy should also be changed to reflect the "new realities." Although American aid had successfully stimulated economic growth and industrial output in some countries, the House Committee on Foreign Affairs lamented that the gains "have not been adequately or equitably distributed to the poor majority in those countries," and that massive social and economic problems prevented the large majority of people in other nations from breaking out of the "vicious circle of poverty which plagues most developing countries." (US Code Congressional and Administrative News, 1973: 2811). The Act asserted that henceforth American aid would depend less on large-scale capital transfers for physical infrastructure and industrial expansion, as it had in the past, and more on transferring technical expertise, modest financial assistance and agricultural and industrial goods to meet "critical development problems." Aid would be used to promote changes that affect the lives of the majority of people in developing countries: in food production, rural development, nutritional standards, population planning, health and educational services, public administration and human resource development.

The World Bank, at the same time, reordered its priorities and procedures. In his address to the Board of Governors in 1973, Robert S. McNamara also noted that the benefits of international aid had not filtered down to the majority of the poor. He insisted that the Bank increase investments in those sectors and areas of the world where they would have the greatest impact on raising the productivity and income of "nearly 800 million individuals − 40 percent out of a total of two billion − [who] survive on income estimated at 30 cents a day and in conditions of malnutrition, illiteracy and squalor." He challenged the Bank to design "new style" projects for achieving growth-with-equity and called for rapid increases in the amount of loans for agricultural and social projects made to the Bank's poorest members. A new emphasis would be placed on loans for multi-purpose, integrated, low-cost, replicable projects designed to benefit the poorest groups by increasing the productive capacity of small-scale farmers and rural industries. He called for a comprehensive program for alleviating poverty in rural areas. Such a program would require, among other things, more rapid land and tenancy reform, better access for the poor to credit, expansion of potable water supplies, extension of technical assistance to subsistence farmers, greater access by the poor to public services, "and most critical of all, new forms of rural institutions and organizations that will give as much attention to promoting the inherent potential and productivity of the poor as is generally given to protecting the power of the privileged." (McNamara, 1973: 10).

Similarly, United Nations Specialized Agencies, such as the International Labor Office (ILO) began calling for new employment-generating strategies that would help the world's poor to satisfy their "basic human needs." In its Declaration of Principles, the World Employment Conference organized by ILO in 1976, argued that "past development strategies in most developing countries have not led to the eradication of poverty and unemployment," and that "major shifts in development strategies at both national and international levels are urgently needed in order to ensure full employment and an adequate income" for the majority of the poor in the developing world as quickly as possible. Development plans and assistance policies, it asserted, should focus on providing for the minimum private consumption and community service needs of the poor and on promoting full employment as a way of generating the income required by the poor to satisfy those needs (International Labor Office, 1976: 5–6).

Previous assistance policies were attacked not only for their ineffectiveness in promoting economic progress but also because they reinforced those arrangements in the international economic system that worked to the disadvantage of poor countries. Development assistance was seen by many Third World political leaders as an extension of colonialism and imperialism. It was designed to attain the economic and political objectives of rich countries rather than to alleviate poverty or promote growth in developing nations.

In 1980 the Brandt Commission warned of dire consequences for the future of mankind unless a new international economic order could be forged to reduce the growing gap in income and wealth between rich and poor societies (Independent Commission on International Development, 1980). But drastic changes in the international economy at the beginning of the 1980s illustrated more forcefully the degree of uncertainty and complexity that is inherent in development problems. International economic recession raised serious doubts about the ability of international organizations and governments in developing countries to promote or sustain high rates of economic growth and created formidable financial obstacles to ameliorating widespread poverty. Deep recession and slow growth in Western industrial economies had world-wide effects – raising interest rates on investment capital, reducing demand for the exports of developing countries, and increasing the costs of their imports. The rapidly rising price of petroleum – an 80 percent increase between 1978 and 1980 alone – had devastating effects on the economies of oil-importing countries, which included most of the world's poorest nations. Debt service rose to unprecedented levels in many developing countries, placing strains on already meager development budgets and threatening the survival of many of the projects and programs that had begun during the late 1970s. International financial assistance to developing nations decreased sharply at a time when the need for additional resources was becoming more urgent (World Bank, 1981).

World Bank (1981: iii) officials predicted that even under optimistic international economic conditions "the income gap between the richest and poorest countries will continue to increase" and that if pessimistic projections prevail "the number of individuals living in absolute poverty will rise." Again, trends in international assistance policy and development strategy in developing countries changed. Stronger emphasis was placed on reforming the economic structure in developing nations to adjust to price increases for imports and to declining demand for exports. The concern with alleviating poverty and increasing the income and living conditions of the poorest groups began to wane. Many of the human resource development programs that were found to be essential to sustained economic growth during the 1970s were labelled "welfare" policies by conservative economists who gained prominence during the early 1980s, and were subordinated to private-sector production-oriented strategies.

CHANGING POLICIES, AND CONVENTIONAL PERSPECTIVES ON PLANNING AND IMPLEMENTATION

Although these changes in development policies and aid strategies were strongly influenced by rapidly changing international economic conditions and evolving theories of economic development, they failed to reflect lessons about the nature of development problems. Assumptions about how policy planning and implementation should be done were never seriously re-examined. The methods of planning and administration employed by governments in developing countries and international assistance organizations have nearly always been inappropriate to the nature of development problems. They more often obstructed or constrained rather than facilitated and encouraged experimentation and social learning. Leaders of developing countries and officials of international assistance agencies have more readily acknowledged the complexity and uncertainty of development problems in recent years and modified their policies and programs as they learned from experience. But their analytical and administrative procedures have yet to come to grips with the experimental nature of development policies and with the uncertainties of development theories.

In a critique of the Brandt Commission report issued in 1980, former World Bank official P. D. Henderson (1980: 16) highlighted the discrepancies between prescription and reality that plagued nearly all policy statements on international development problems. He pointed out that the Brandt report "embodies a high degree of confidence that the future either is or can be predictable and controllable." He noted that "too little account is taken of the pervasive and irreducible uncertainty which surrounds the future, nor would one gather from the Report that much of the uncertainty that could in principle be reduced arises from the behavior of governments." International assistance organizations continued to assume that their policies, programs and projects could be rationally conceived and comprehensively planned solutions to development problems. Henderson's reaction to the Brandt Commission report was one of the few to challenge its assumptions about the certainty of development problems and to question whether "the issues of social and economic life are such that it makes sense to think in terms of 'solutions' to them – as though they were like the entries in a crossword puzzle, for which there can be found a recognized, uniquely correct, and permanently valid set of responses."

In reality, development planners and officials of international lending institutions had been attempting to promote social and economic change in developing societies since the early 1940s with relatively little knowledge of the conditions they were seeking to transform and with little certainty that their theories, policies and projects would produce the desired effects. Indeed, neither the array of factors causing poverty and underdevelopment nor the dynamics of economic growth have ever been fully understood.

The only certainty to emerge from past experience is that development problems are extremely complex, differing drastically among societies and over time. Policies pursued successfully in one country do not necessarily work in others, and conditions that promoted or obstructed economic and social change in some societies do not prevail in all. The export industrialization policies that successfully promoted economic growth in Taiwan and South Korea during the 1960s and early 1970s, for instance, could not be replicated later in other Asian countries. China's successful programs for providing basic human needs and promoting a more equitable distribution of income during the 1950s and 1960s could not achieve similar results in other socialist countries. Indeed, they were abandoned by China for different strategies when new political philosophies emerged during the late 1970s and early 1980s.

Widely varying values, ideologies, attitudes and behavior of people and governments in developing nations have made it impossible to define development objectives universally. And although some economic and social problems were found to be common to many poor countries they also differed in significant ways, making general solutions inappropriate to any particular nation. Even global influences such as inflation, rising prices for factors of production and changing patterns of international trade affected different countries in different ways.

The success of economic development policies in the future is likely to depend on the resolution of two basic issues. One is how developing nations can mobilize and use their own resources more effectively to increase the productivity and income of millions of people living in poverty. Ultimately this may prove to be far more important than increasing the flow of financial and technical assistance from rich countries or redirecting patterns of international trade. The other issue is how governments and international assistance institutions can organize their planning and administrative procedures to cope more effectively with the growing complexity and uncertainty of development problems. The two issues are related and both are examined in this book.

The focus of the book, however, is less on the substance of development policies and more on processes and methods by which programs and projects are formulated and implemented. The disjunction that exists between the nature of development problems and the methods of policy planning and implementation used by governments and international agencies has been an important factor accounting for the disappointing results of development programs in the past and its impact will even be more serious in the future.

PUBLIC POLICY-MAKING AS SOCIAL EXPERIMENTATION

The experimental nature of development policies becomes more evident when the history of development theories and aid policies is viewed, as it is in chapter 2, from a perspective different from that underlying conventional development theory and when public policy-making is recognized as an incremental process of trial and error through political interaction and successive approximation (Lindblom, 1965; Rondinelli, 1975; Wildavsky, 1979). As Johnston and Clark (1982: 11) in their review of rural development programs point out, the commonly held perception of the development problem differs substantially from reality:

> To speak of the "development problem" is to imply a well structured world of unambiguous objectives, mutually exclusive choices,

authoritative decision-makers and willing decision-endurers. In contrast to this idyllic vision, development actually involves a staggering variety of people and organizations all pulling and pushing and otherwise interacting with each other in pursuit of their various interests. Since each actor in this process has a more or less unique perspective on "the development problem," the policy process invariably deals with numerous overlapping problems, or in Ackoff's phrase, a "mess." Turning messes into problems about which something constructive can be done is one way of viewing the central task of policy analysis.

Such perceptions of the dynamics of development suggest a far different approach to policy analysis, planning and implementation than is usually prescribed by those who hold a rational, intellectually guided or technocratic view of problem-solving. "The planning model recognizes that implementation may fail because the original plan was infeasible. But it does not recognize the important point that many – perhaps most – constraints remain hidden in the planning stage, and are only discovered in the implementation process," Majone and Wildavsky (1978: 106) point out. This view implies that few programs and projects can be designed in great detail and carried out in highly coordinated and controlled fashion in accordance with comprehensive plans. "When problems are puzzles for which unique solutions exist, technicians can take over," Majone and Wildavsky contend (p. 113). "But when problems are defined through the process of attempting to draft acceptable solutions, then analysts become creators as well as implementors of policy." Under conditions of complex interaction and uncertainty development policies, programs and projects can, at best, be designed to isolate small, manageable aspects of problems and to intervene in what seem to be strategically important ways to cope with them incrementally.

Since the ability of development planners to predict and control the outcomes of their programs and projects under conditions of uncertainty is quite limited, their methods of analysis, planning and management must be better suited to recognizing and dealing with uncertainty, detecting and correcting errors, generating and using knowledge as experiments progress, and modifying actions as opportunities and constraints appear during implementation. It will be shown later that few of the planning and management techniques now used by governments and international assistance agencies meet these needs. Instead, many suppress social learning and constrain experimentation.

DESIGNING AND ORGANIZING PROJECTS AS POLICY EXPERIMENTS

It is the uncertainties and complexities of development policies that must become the major concern of development planners and project designers. Although little can – or should – be done to try to uncover and control them all at the outset of a project, the degree of uncertainty and ignorance involved in pursuing policies should be realistically assessed. Attempts to plan in more detailed and precise fashion should proceed incrementally only as uncertainties or unknowns are reduced or clarified during implementation. Planning must be viewed as an incremental process of testing propositions about the most effective means of coping with social problems and of reassessing and redefining both the problems and the projects as more is learned about their complexities and about the economic, social and political factors affecting the outcome of proposed courses of action. Complex social experiments can be partially guided but never fully controlled. Thus, methods of analysis and procedures of implementation must be flexible and incremental, facilitating social interaction so that those groups most directly affected by a problem can search for and pursue mutually acceptable objectives. Rather than providing a blueprint for action, planning should facilitate continuous learning and interaction, allowing policy-makers and managers to readjust and modify programs and projects as more is learned about the conditions with which they are trying to cope (Korten, 1980; Korten and Alfonso, 1981). Planning and implementation must be regarded as mutually dependent activities that refine and improve each other over time, rather than as separate functions.

If, in fact, all development activities are essentially experimental, fundamental changes are needed in the way governments and international assistance agencies formulate policies and implement projects.

First, it is highly unlikely that uncertain, experimental activities can be planned comprehensively and designed in great detail at the outset. As will be seen in chapters 2 and 3, a variety of economic, social and political forces operate in developing nations to make detailed planning difficult or impossible. Lack of knowledge about the groups and societies for which projects are proposed makes detailed design ineffective or perverse. Inability to control processes of interaction that affect the success of projects makes attempts at comprehensive planning costly and inefficient. Pressures to make administrators and managers conform to preconceived designs constrain them from taking appropriate action to deal with unanticipated difficulties as they arise.

The experience in developing countries that is described in chapter 3 indicates that Third World planners and administrators have had as much difficulty applying quantitative, systematic and comprehensive techniques of analysis, planning and management as those in Western industrial countries. The growing criticisms of cost-benefit analysis, planning-programming-and-budgeting systems, critical-path methods of scheduling, quantitative model building and management systems when they are applied to social or political problems in Western countries are based not only on their inappropriateness, but also on their ineffectiveness. The dangers of transferring them to the Third World are exacerbated by the reluctance of experts to inform planners and administrators in developing countries of their limitations. A long list of criticisms of quantitative analyses and systems management has been compiled by social scientists in Western industrial countries (Wildavsky, 1969; Schick, 1973; Sapolski, 1972; Hoos, 1972). Among the most important criticisms are that:

[margin note: Criticism of quant analy. in Devel. Admin.]

1 Systems analyses require a concise definition of goals and objectives, but the goals of social programs and policies often cannot be clearly defined because they are really expressions of social values on which various groups usually disagree and which cannot be stated in purely economic terms;

2 There are severe problems in quantifying and measuring the results or effects of public programs because there is often no physical product associated with them;

3 Identifying and categorizing inputs, outputs, costs and benefits is a subjective rather than an objective process on which analysts and interest groups often disagree;

4 Government agencies at all levels, even in Western industrialized countries, lack the administrative capacity and analytical talent to do these types of analyses effectively;

5 Obtaining adequate and reliable data on which to base systems analysis and synoptic planning is difficult at best and often impossible, especially within bureaucracies in which administrators view such analyses as a threat to their political influence;

6 Systems analyses often ignore or discount the complex processes of social interaction through which decisions are really made, processes that are based on incremental and disjointed decision-making through bargaining, exchange and compromise;

7 Political leaders often either do not understand or are unwilling to accept the results of systems analysis and comprehensive planning and therefore tend to ignore them in arriving at decisions;

8 Because the programs or policy options subjected to systems analysis are usually different in their objectives, characteristics, purposes and content it is usually very difficult or impossible to make relevant comparisons and trade-offs among them or to deal with the "crossover" problems of treating as coherent programs similar activities that are the responsibility of different agencies and organizations;

9 Systems analysis and comprehensive planning are often ineffective because they are episodic and time consuming, whereas political decision-making is continuous or cyclical and requires immediate and continuing inputs of information; and,

10 Systems analyses are usually addressed to questions of how to maximize the utilities of individual decision-makers whereas policy-making is primarily concerned with questions of how to distribute public resources to groups with different goals and purposes in the most politically effective way.

The criticisms of technocratic methods, and especially of cost-benefit analysis, in Western industrial countries thus arise not only from the great difficulty in operationalizing them when they are applied to social issues, but also because they are largely incompatible with the way political decisions are made. Moreover, they discourage analysts from understanding the complexity and uncertainty of the problems they are dealing with. Meltsner (1976: 32) noted in his study of policy analysts in the United States that they are ineffective precisely because they try to clarify and make technical those issues that are inherently complex and political. "What the technician shuns, the politician embraces," he points out. Benveniste (1972: 70) argues that the requirements of systems analysis are often irreconcilable with political requirements:

Goal specification requires a high level of political consensus. When social consensus exists goal specificity does not create political costs. When many divergent views exist, however, the possibility of establishing well-defined goals that satisfy everyone becomes much more difficult. Even the process of spelling out goals may result in considerable conflict as each contending faction struggles to place its own preferences high on the list of objectives. Vague and ill defined goals are an equivalent to having secret goals. As long as goals are secret, it is possible for competing groups to pursue their own ends without necessarily encroaching on each other.

Other critics question whether systems analysis in fact leads to a more reflective and systematic process of decision-making. Peter Self

(1975: 91–2) has denied both the logic and the assumptions of what he calls the "myth of numerology," or the belief that "rationality equals counting and measuring." He denies that quantification necessarily causes policy-makers to think more carefully or broadly about the factors influencing the outcome of a decision, or that it is even a necessary condition for deliberation and reflection. "The critical question here is how carefully and widely an individual is prepared to think about his decision premises," Self contends. "If he thinks in a narrow way numerology will not make him reflective, and if he is reflective there is no need for numerology."

The greater danger is that systems approaches encourage analysts to think more narrowly, to consider only what is quantifiable and to reduce uncertain and complex conditions to abstract or unrealistic assumptions merely to fit a deductive model. Moreover, Self (p. 93) argues that in many cost-benefit analyses the "fixing of eyes upon the techniques of final evaluation shifts attention from the intervening process and the reasoning behind them. The conclusions become numerate but shallow." The point is underlined by former US Secretary of Defense James Schlesinger (1968: 282) when he notes that "the availability of analytical tools may obscure the unpleasant reality that many public policy problems are highly intractable. The real problem, he argues, "is not method but understanding; the linking of costs and benefits is only as good as man's knowledge. Yet there exists an image of systems analysis in which expert practitioners apply their methods and grind out solutions to policy problems – in the absence of a deep knowledge of the relevant social institutions or real world mechanics."

In their review of experience with rural development in Third World countries, Johnston and Clark (1982: 231) argue that cost-benefit analysis and quantitative models have been applicable to a very small number of routine and tactical problems and that they have proven to be "of little value in guiding the strategic debate over, for example, the priority that should be given to nutrition, health and family planning programs or the choice between unimodal and bimodal agricultural development." Bromley and Bustelo (1982) emphasize the dangers of transferring such techniques to developing countries in Latin America without providing planners and administrators with substantial information about their limitations and inappropriate applications. They complain that much of the technocratic methodology was introduced in Latin America simply to satisfy the requirements of international aid agencies and not from local perceptions of its usefulness. Prescriptions for the adoption of cost-benefit analysis and management systems continue because international development banks and powerful groups of national consultants support and require them, "enabling technocratic firms to make substantial profits by selling their sophisticated expertise and their knowledge of the latest techniques."

But even if such techniques could be made operational, the complex and uncertain nature of social problems makes it impossible to anticipate, analyze and control all of the variables that affect development projects. Hirschman is correct in his conclusion that if planners of most of the World Bank projects that he observed had been able to anticipate all of the problems that later befell them, few of the projects would have been judged to be feasible and actually undertaken. Yet, creative managers were often able to cope with unanticipated obstacles by redesigning projects as they progressed and to accommodate to constraints and opportunities as they arose. "The term 'implementation' understates the complexity of the task of carrying out projects that are affected by a high degree of initial ignorance and uncertainty," Hirschman (1967: 35) contends. "Here project implementation may often mean in fact a long voyage of discovery in the most varied domains, from technology to politics."

If that voyage is to be successful, the methods used to formulate and carry out development projects must encourage the process of discovery and use information and experience to chart a course of action along the way. This implies that planning and implementation must be more closely integrated and that project design must proceed through a series of stages in order to reduce uncertainties and unknowns: from highly experimental activities that probe possible courses of action to pilot and demonstration projects that test alternatives and identify conditions under which interventions are more or less effective. Some experimental and pilot projects may lead to full-scale production projects that can be widely replicated and administered through more conventional procedures. Others may be found to be useful only under particular conditions and not replicated, or to be inappropriate or ineffective and abandoned.

As will be seen in chapter 4, *experimental projects* are needed when little is known about problems or the most effective means of setting objectives. Unknowns and uncertainties affect nearly all aspects of development projects, from the definition of problems and the feasibility of alternative interventions to the choice of the most appropriate technologies and organizational arrangements. Although experimentation is quite common in agricultural and health projects, much less attention has been given to experiments in other fields of human development. In most projects that are sponsored by governments and international agencies – specially those undertaken in rural areas – little is initially known about the conditions or needs of the intended beneficiaries, their attitudes and behavior or the social and political environment in which projects must be implemented. Nor is much known about appropriate types, magnitudes and combinations of resources needed to deal with development problems in many countries, the most effective timing and sequencing of activities, or the best production and delivery systems for intended beneficiaries. International agencies and governments of developing countries have relatively little experience with designing and carrying out development projects as experimental activities, but what little they do have suggests that such projects should be small in scale. They sometimes can be carried out by generalists, but they often require technically trained staff. In any case, they must elicit the participation of potential beneficiaries in the design and organizational phases, their managers must have easy access to specialized inputs and resources, and methods of implementation must be flexible (Hapgood, 1965; Lele, 1975). Experimental projects must often be isolated or sheltered from routine administrative responsibilities and from political pressures to replicate them too soon or to abandon them too early. In chapter 4 it will be argued that conventional forms of scientific experimentation are not appropriate for most development projects and that other, less formal, processes of social experimentation must be tried.

Pilot projects can be used to test the results of experiments under a greater variety of conditions and to adapt and modify methods, technologies or procedures that have proven to be effective in other countries to local conditions and needs. It will be seen in chapter 4 that pilot projects are most appropriate when the problem or objective of a policy is well defined or when much is already known about the effects of small-scale experiments. Pilot projects are usually intended to test new methods and technology, determine their relevance, transferability and acceptability and to explore alternative ways of disseminating results or of delivering goods and services. The relatively few studies that have been done of pilot projects suggests that careful attention must be given to choosing appropriate locations, structuring activities to fit local needs and conditions, collecting baseline data and, especially, monitoring and evaluating the project to determine conditions that influence success or failure. The projects must be evaluated in such a way that preconditions for replication and successful demonstration can also be determined. Pilot projects must also be organized to shelter their managers from undue political pressures to show quick results since implementation is still primarily by trial and error, requiring creative and flexible administration.

When pilot phases have been completed, *demonstration projects* can be used to exhibit the effectiveness and to increase the acceptability of new methods, techniques or forms of social interaction on a broader scale. Although they may be less risky and uncertain than experimental and pilot projects, innovative and creative management is still required for gaining acceptance of new ways of doing things. Experience with agricultural, family planning, rural development and small-scale industrial projects in Africa and Latin America clearly indicates that successful demonstrations must be profitable to participants, novel and innovative, yet related to their experience. Demonstration projects should include all components required to support successful adaptations, be relatively simple to understand and make use of accessible materials and tools. Moreover, they must be highly visible, produce results that are easy to explain and be replicable with a minimum of supervision and training (Hapgood, 1965; Shaefer-Kehnert, 1977; Rondinelli, 1979a).

Replication, diffusion or production projects should evolve from experimental, pilot and demonstration phases. Widespread replication and full production can be undertaken when some of the uncertainties and unknowns have been dealt with, or when a great deal is already known about the elements or potential impact of a project that would ordinarily be tested in experimental, pilot and demonstration activities. A primary concern in planning and implementing these projects is to test full-scale production technology and to organize an effective delivery system for disseminating results or distributing outputs.

It must be kept in mind, however, that *all* development projects are somewhat experimental and that even seemingly routine replications often meet unanticipated difficulties when projects are transferred from one setting to another.

The perception of development policies as experimental activities implies that new forms of analysis, planning and administration must be devised that are better suited to experimentation and to uncovering and coping with the uncertainties and risks attending policy implementation. An adaptive approach to development administration is outlined in chapter 5. The greater the degree of uncertainty and the larger the number of unknowns involved in a proposed course of action, the more flexible and probing the methods of analysis – and the more adjustable the procedures of implementation – must be. In chapter 5 it is argued that the objectives of planning should not be to control in fine detail the activities that will be pursued during implementation, but to increase the probabilities that appropriate action can and will be taken as more is learned about problems, constraints and opportunities as a project progresses.

Indeed, the perception of development activities offered in the following chapters suggests that a primary purpose of projects should be to build up gradually the planning and administrative capabilities of people and organizations in developing nations rather than simply spending larger amounts of money to build yet another highway or factory for them. By designing and organizing projects to reduce uncertainties and unknowns incrementally, integrate planning and implementation, and use the acquired knowledge to alter and modify courses of action during execution, projects will become more effective instruments of learning that can make a greater contribution to development in the future.

2

Development policies as social experiments

A review of the evolution of economic development theories and aid strategies since the 1940s yields three propositions that support the arguments set out in chapter 1. First, development theories have evolved from a complex process of social learning and political interaction. Second, the methods of planning and implementation used by governments and international agencies have rarely been appropriate for dealing with the complexities and uncertainties inherent in development problems. Third, planning and administrative procedures that governments and international organizations used to formulate and implement physical development projects in the past are particularly unsuited to human resource, growth-with-equity and poverty alleviation strategies.[1]

The complex and uncertain changes that have come about in development policies and aid strategies can be seen in three major periods in the history of development theories. The industrial development policies of the 1950s and early 1960s sought maximum growth in the economies of developing nations and assumed that trickle down and spread effects would incorporate the majority of the poor into productive economic activities. The policies sought rapid and high rates of growth in national output with little concern for distributive effects, and thus used largely untargetted aid strategies.

Development policies of the 1960s were designed to overcome obstacles and eliminate bottlenecks to economic growth by redistributing productive assets, developing human resources, controlling population growth, and increasing productive capacity in lagging sectors of developing economies. Sectoral development plans sought to change those social and economic conditions that were considered to be obstacles to development. These policies used semi-targetted aid: technical and financial assistance was more focused and concentrated on specific development problems and on groups of people with characteristics thought to be adverse to economic growth.

The policies of the 1970s sought economic growth with social equity;

they were concerned as much with the distribution of benefits as with the rate and pace of economic output. They sought to channel aid to the poor majority and resources to subsistence populations in rural areas, provide for basic human needs in the poorest countries, and improve the living standards of "special publics" or groups of the poor. These objectives were largely pursued through targetted aid strategies.

Turbulent changes in the world economy and in the economic, social and political conditions within developing nations in the early 1980s created an environment of greater uncertainty, in which the objectives and approaches to foreign assistance changed quickly. A new emphasis was placed on macro-economic adjustments to the rising cost of imports for developing nations and lower demand for their exports. Greater attention was given to private sector productivity. Less resources were available for international assistance, and the strong emphasis on meeting the needs and increasing the productivity of the poor that had characterized development theories in the previous decade began to wane.

GROWTH MAXIMIZATION AND TRICKLE DOWN POLICIES

When the Point Four Program, or Marshall Plan, was proposed in the 1940s, the intention of aid-giving nations was to rebuild the physical and industrial structure of countries that had attained relatively high levels of productive capacity prior to World War II. International aid programs sought to rehabilitate physical infrastructure and industrial plant, temporarily feed large numbers of people displaced from their jobs by the war, and re-establish market systems in European nations. Other international funding arrangements established in the wake of the Marshall Plan had similar objectives. The World Bank's mission, for instance, was clearly reflected in the organization's formal title – the International Bank for Reconstruction and Development – and in the order in which the elements of the title appear. Concern for promoting development in poor countries was subordinate to reconstructing productive capacity in more economically advanced nations that had been devastated in a long and intense global conflict. In the late 1940s and early 1950s the emphasis of aid-giving organizations was on macro-economic development, national planning, and construction of capital intensive industries, highways and power generating systems, and on rebuilding the financial capacity of European countries to invest in their own reconstruction. The plans called for large-scale and expensive projects requiring sophisticated engineering skills and high technology equipment. The governments receiving aid were generally experienced in industrial development, had well-trained professionals and skilled workers, high levels of planning and managerial capability and a strong motivation to recover as quickly as possible (Mikesell, 1968; Mason and Asher, 1973).

As success was achieved in rehabilitating the economies of Europe, bilateral and international aid organizations turned their attention increasingly to poorer nations of the world that had never attained high levels of industrial production. Their economic, social and political characteristics were quite different from those of European nations as were the motivations of their leaders and the extent of poverty within their populations. Preconditions for economic growth that were taken for granted in European nations did not exist in most countries of the Third World.

But international aid agencies pursued much the same strategies in poor countries as they had used successfully in reconstructing the economies of Europe. Little attention was given during the 1950s to differences in conditions and needs in the Third World until these conditions appeared to create obstacles to achieving high levels of industrial output. A strong belief that the same processes of industrialization that brought economic growth to Europe would bring growth and modernization to developing nations was pervasive in aid organizations. So was the confidence of development theorists that the benefits of growth would eventually reach the vast majority of people in poor countries through automatic market mechanisms and spread and trickle down effects. Thus, the need to channel aid to the poor was obviated.

The industrialization policies prescribed by macro-economic development theorists during the 1950s and 1960s sought rapid increases in gross national product (GNP). The only real debate over these policies concerned the means by which they would be achieved. Some theorists argued that the most effective way of attaining high levels of economic growth was through heavy investment in capital-intensive industry as a "leading sector." Others contended that a "big push" was needed in all sectors at the same time to increase output and demand for industrial production. Both theories were modeled on processes of economic growth that occurred in Western Europe and North America during the second half of the nineteenth and first half of the twentieth centuries. Developing nations were urged to seek large amounts of foreign capital, promote specialization in low-wage or raw material oriented industries, and apply capital-intensive technology to the production process. Export and import substitution industries were usually favored. As industrial output grew it would generate more employment and higher incomes. They in turn would raise the level of demand for agricultural and industrial goods, increase savings, allow for expanded capital formation and generate new investment. Public expenditures, bolstered by foreign aid, would be concentrated in building physical infrastructure that would lower production costs and improve distribution. Nearly three-quarters of the loans made by the World Bank and International Development Association from 1946 to 1963 were made for physical infrastructure projects, especially for transportation, electrical power, ports and harbors and industrial plants.

One group of economists − leading sector theorists − insisted that the most effective means of generating and sustaining high levels of economic growth was by investing heavily in a single sector. Industry was usually considered the "engine of growth" for developing economies, but some economists argued that other sectors might be more appropriate for initiating investment. Some, such as Arthur Lewis (1954; 1955) and Theodore Schultz (1964), noted that agricultural investment would provide income for industrialization in rural nations. Still others, such as Currie (1966) insisted that growth in housing and consumer goods sectors would stimulate demand for industrial products and set off the spiral of investment.

But many economists such as Albert Hirschman (1959) maintained that it mattered little which sector was chosen initially because heavy investment in any sector would generate increased demand and induced investment in all other sectors. Growth in the leading sector would spread and thereby raise the overall level of economic output. Hirschman argued that heavy public investments in either directly productive or social overhead activities would lower costs, and through complementarities in the economy, create increased demand and pressures for mobilization and investment of private capital. The ripple effect from this initial stimulation would generate growth throughout the economy. Thus, the objective of leading sector theorists was to create a set of continuous tensions in the economy: a sequence of events that "leads away from equilibrium is precisely the ideal pattern of development," Hirschman (1959: 66) insisted. Unbalanced growth would generate and enlist resources and abilities for development that had previously been "hidden, scattered or badly utilized." The mechanisms by which growth would spread were thought to be largely automatic once investment began. "If such a chain of unbalanced growth sequences could be set up," Hirschman (1959: 72) predicted, "the economic policy makers could just watch the proceedings from the sidelines."

Other economists seeking maximum economic growth argued for a different approach. They noted that in labor surplus economies investment in one industry or set of industries could not generate sufficient employment, income and demand to absorb output. Moreover, heavy investment in one industry precluded development of other sectors that provide inputs for industry. They argued that massive amounts of foreign aid should be used in combination with national resources to make a "big push" for development by investing simultaneously in all sectors. Balanced investment would create the internal complementarities that Hirschman and others assumed already existed in developing economies. It would allow each sector to supply the others without heavy reliance on imports. Appropriate use could therefore be made of natural resources, employment would increase throughout the economy at the same time, and greater demand would be created for outputs in each sector. Agriculture and commerce would benefit as well as manufacturing. Moreover, expansion of industry would proceed at pace with improvements in labor skills and entrepreneurial experience. Investment in physical infrastructure, public utilities, production equipment and plant would be balanced, but sizeable enough in each sector to push the economy into a stage of rapid and sustained growth. Such a strategy was necessary, Nurkse (1953) insisted, because in the long run productive capacity, level of production and ability to use capital to increase output were all limited by the size of the market, which was extremely small in most poor countries.

The question of how massive poverty – a major factor limiting the size of markets in developing nations – would be alleviated, was rarely asked by development theorists or directly addressed in aid strategy. The problem of reducing the large gaps in income and wealth between rich and poor nations would be solved, Rosenstein-Rodan (1943) argued, by achieving "a more equal distribution of income between different areas of the world by raising incomes in depressed areas at a higher rate than in the rich areas." This would occur internationally through the same automatic mechanisms that Hirschman relied upon in national economies. Investment in any activity would set in motion complementary activities that would spread growth throughout the economic system, thereby eventually alleviating poverty.

As industrial production increased in developing countries new jobs would be created, demand for new products would be expanded, and through forward, backward and lateral linkages new investments would be made. This would create additional employment opportunities and raise overall levels of income. Some of the new income would be spent on basic needs for food, shelter, education and health, and some would be taxed to provide public services, and some would be saved and reinvested. Not only would increasing employment draw larger numbers of people into the productive system, but also the resulting demand for labor, goods and services would spread from the major urban centers where large-scale industries were located, into smaller towns and rural areas. Increasing incomes would create higher demand for agricultural goods and the application of new technology by farmers would make agriculture more productive and less labor-intensive. Surplus agricultural labor would be absorbed in the expanding industrial sector. As agricultural production increased, profits would be reinvested in more efficient technology, better seed varieties, irrigation and other inputs that would generate even higher yields with less labor and land. Once the economy reached the "take-off" stage (Rostow, 1952), more of the poor would begin to benefit and a growth cycle would generate higher levels of output, create incentives for diversification and allow more technologically advanced industries to succeed low-wage and raw material oriented industries.

Many economists believed, along with Kuznets (1966) who formalized the theory, that in the initial stages of growth the largest share of income would go to higher income groups, but as growth continued the poor's relative share of income would increase. When growth was rapid enough to change the dualistic structure of the economy, a more equitable distribution of benefits would begin to eliminate destitution. Many economists argued that reallocation of investments to generate a wider distribution of income by channeling aid to poor groups in developing societies would slow the overall rate of economic growth and thus delay the time at which the poor's share of income would begin to rise on the "Kuznets curve."

RELIANCE ON LONG-RANGE, CENTRALIZED, NATIONAL PLANNING

Both the leading sector and big-push theories relied on comprehensive, long-range planning by national governments to formulate and implement development policies. Macro-economic planning became the main instrument for achieving growth policies and a precondition for international aid to poor countries.

Macro-economic planning became fashionable following World War II. Although pre-war experiments were not uncommon, they were limited, and prompted mostly by the Soviet Union's apparent success in mobilizing investment resources through central planning and by European governments' attempts to "rationalize" and control colonial economies in the developing world. The spread of national planning in the late 1940s and early 1950s can be more directly attributed to the effectiveness of war mobilization planning in Europe and to the desire of governments attaining post-war political independence for rapid economic growth. But perhaps the greatest impetus to national planning was the insistence of international aid agencies that grants and loans be made in conformance with coherent plans for national development. Thus, serious attempts to plan and manage economies came in the wake of World Bank Economic Missions to developing countries in the 1950s. Creation of the Colombo Plan at about the same time provided additional incentives for national planning in India, Pakistan, Singapore and Sarawak. Attempts in the early 1960s by United States aid officials to mandate national planning as a precondition for assistance, stimulated such efforts in Korea, the Philippines and Taiwan (Mason and Asher, 1973; Waterston, 1965).

The influence of international lending agencies and economic theorists was reflected clearly, for instance, in the objectives and procedures adopted by Asian planners. Although national planning evolved in different ways in different political systems, its goals and procedures nonetheless manifested striking similarities. "The basic principle in the ideology of economic planning," Myrdal (1970: 175), noted in his extensive study of Southeast Asia, "is that the state shall take an active, indeed, the decisive role in the economy; by its own acts of investment and enterprise, and by its various controls – inducements and restrictions – over the private sector the state shall initiate, spur and steer economic development." Policies thus would be "rationally coordinated, and the coordination [made] explicit in an overall plan for a number of years ahead."

For most countries attempting to establish political and economic independence following the war, central planning offered not only an efficient tool for allocating scarce resources, but also a symbol of progress and self-control. By the mid-1960s Waterston (1965: 28) could observe with little exaggeration that "the national plan appears to have joined the national anthem and the national flag as a symbol of sovereignty and modernity." But beyond mere symbolism, Asians turned to central planning as a means of quickly achieving their economic and political aspirations. Most of Asia's early plans reflected goals similar to those of Malaysia's first Five-Year Plan. Drafted in 1954 with the assistance of the World Bank Economic Mission, it sought to stimulate industrialization, expand public facilities and infrastructure, and create employment for a growing labor force. Through national planning the government would rapidly accelerate public and private investment, especially in export industries, and increase the rates of capital formation and savings (Rudner, 1975). Similarly, countries like Ceylon turned to national planning not only to expand employment, but also to increase exports and balance foreign payments, diversify domestic production and generate higher levels of national income (Government of Ceylon, 1959).

In other countries, such as Indonesia, which initiated its eight-year development plan in the late 1950s, central planning was an instrument of nation-building in the post-colonial period. President Sukarno designed a plan aimed at increasing consumption, self-sufficiency in food and clothing production, and basic infrastructure and utilities. Promoting self-sufficiency in basic commodities was motivated more by political than economic concerns, resulting from Sukarno's desire to disassociate Indonesia from its colonial past and to evoke self-sacrifice, political support and national solidarity among a diverse people (Humphrey, 1962). As the ideology of national planning spread, Asian governments assigned to it increasingly complex and diverse objectives but the major goals remained those of accelerating investment and the growth of gross national product.

During the 1950s and 1960s Asian national planning took three basic forms: (1) top-down planning, through which a central planning agency formulated policies based on macro-economic, quantitative models for the national economy; (2) bottom-up planning, through which the central planning agency compiled and reviewed the investment proposals of national ministries, local governments and semi-public corporations and allocated resources to them on the basis of centrally determined economic priorities; and (3) mixed systems, which used a combination of top-down and bottom-up approaches.

Top-down planning usually began with designation of broad national development goals and targets. Macro-economic analyses and econometric models sought to forecast long-range conditions and – based on predictions concerning operation of the economy and the influence of exogenous variables – to compare development objectives with forecasted conditions. Investment resources were then allocated to sectors with projected shortfalls. Macro-economic studies, the formulation of alternative targets and strategies, and preliminary design of the national plan, were usually the responsibility of a central planning agency, reporting to the prime minister or a council of ministers. The final plan, based on initial policy recommendations, tempered by other political and economic factors, sought not only to control public agencies' investment decisions, but also to guide their operating and budgeting decisions as well.

The Korean plans, for instance, in addition to analyzing current economic trends, outlined the content and size of the government fiscal budget and recommended sectoral investment levels and incentives for private enterprise. They attempted to forecast major monetary trends, supplies of and demand for major commodities, foreign capital imports, price fluctuations and significant private sector activities. In addition to establishing targets for public and private investment, the plans set foreign transaction, industrial, population, employment, and science and technology policy for government ministries and publicly controlled institutions (Republic of Korea, 1971). Thailand's development plans during the 1960s were based on econometric models consisting of five functional equations and five identities to project fifteen-year trends in gross domestic product, population, capital formation and savings, imports and exports. Major recommendations for resource allocation and investment policies were based on gaps between desired targets and forecasted conditions (UNDP, 1972).

The bottom-up approach used in other countries began with submission of proposed projects by operating ministries, quasi-public corporations and, sometimes, state, provincial or local governments. In Pakistan, for instance, investment programs originated at the local and provincial levels. Local agencies identified projects which were then reviewed and integrated into sectoral plans by provincial ministries, evaluated and processed by the provincial planning agencies and transmitted to the National Planning Commission for consolidation into a national plan. In India working groups similar to those organized at the national level were formed within State governments to identify, generate and initially formulate investment proposals for inclusion in the national plan (United Nations Economic Commission for Asia and the Far East, 1969).

Still other countries used combinations of bottom-up and top-down planning, or switched from one procedure to the other after evaluating initial results. Some countries such as Thailand used top-down procedures for earlier plans and bottom-up processes later, eventually merging elements of both. The National Economic Development Board (NEDB) in Thailand abandoned econometric modeling in the 1960s and was reorganized to coordinate development policies with operating and budgeting decisions. NEDB was formally charged not only with conducting studies of national socio-economic trends and estimating resource availability, but also with reviewing the investment proposals of various ministries and public agencies. Its staff evaluated potential projects and integrated approved proposals into a national development budget that was submitted to the Council of Ministers for final approval (Changrien, 1970).

The rationale for national planning in nearly all Asian countries was that since the public sector was the dominant force for development in capital-scarce countries, its allocation and investment decisions would have to be rationally, efficiently and objectively planned in order to stimulate the economy. National planning, it was argued, would not only establish a coherent overall framework for public resource allocation, but also establish guidelines for decision-making by public and quasi-public agencies concerned with national development, and provide criteria for evaluating private sector investment.

But Asian experience with national economic planning provided little evidence that it achieved either goal. Economic growth in Asia during the 1950s and 1960s was sporadic and limited to a few countries, and the administration of national economic planning was plagued with severe problems, limiting its usefulness in guiding or controlling investment decisions.

OBSTACLES AND BOTTLENECKS TO DEVELOPMENT

By the early 1960s it became increasingly apparent that in most developing nations a strategy of rapid growth through capital intensive industrialization was not working. Growth occurred in some Third World nations during the 1950s and early 1960s, but at rates well below those sought in national development plans. Studies found that foreign aid had little direct impact on increasing the levels of GNP in less developed countries. Griffin and Enos (1970) discovered, for instance, that the correlation between foreign aid and increases in GNP during the 1950s was weak or insignificant for poor nations in Africa and Asia. Aid and growth were negatively correlated in Latin American countries, where they found that "the greater inflow of capital from abroad, the lower the rate of growth of the receiving country." Governments had difficulty obtaining large amounts of foreign capital to finance ambitious industrialization plans and had little success in mobilizing sufficient savings internally to achieve high rates of capital formation.

Some theorists began questioning the model underlying capital intensive industrialization theories. Dudley Seers (1965), among others, pointed out that the prevailing conditions that made rapid and sustained industrialization possible in Western societies constituted a "special case," and that economic development policies applied successfully under those conditions could not simply be transferred or replicated in developing nations. He noted that in Europe and North America factors of production had been abundant during their periods of industrialization; labor was educated, skilled, mobile and could easily be organized for productive purposes. Land was also abundant, arable and widely held in private ownership. Capital was readily available; most sectors of the economy were heavily capitalized; entrepreneurship was well established; and governments provided inducements for entrepreneurial expansion. The structure of the economy was diversified and dominated by a competitive manufacturing sector that had evolved from numerous cottage and artisan enterprises. Agriculture was largely commercialized at the time of the industrial revolution in these countries and an extensive marketing network had evolved providing farmers with accessible and competitive outlets for their products. Public revenue collection and allocation procedures were firmly established; savings could be mobilized by an efficient banking system; and the level of national investment was already high. Exports were diversified in products for which there was also an internal market. Income distribution was relatively equitable and a comparatively small percentage of the population remained destitute. Population growth was below 2 percent a year and a large percentage of the people lived in urban areas (Hoselitz, 1964).

But in developing countries the conditions were far different. Low levels of education and skills limited the availability of labor for industrial employment. Poor countries lacked large numbers of experienced managers. Low levels of agricultural production and massive poverty in rural areas limited the expansion of internal demand, leaving industries in developing nations at the mercy of export markets in which they were often uncompetitive or at a severe disadvantage. Moreover, poor countries had to pay substantially higher prices for their imports of equipment, technical know-how, intermediate goods and finished products than they received for their exports, leading to serious deficits in their balance of payments. High population growth rates offset advances in output or income, leaving much of the population no better off economically at the end of the 1950s than a decade earlier (Streeten, 1972).

Market mechanisms that were supposed to act as channels for the spread of growth impulses and the filtering down of benefits either did not exist in most developing countries or worked imperfectly. Instead of growth spreading throughout developing economics, resources were often drained from rural hinterlands, through what Myrdal (1957) called "backwash effects," to support industries located in metropolitan centers. Political instability, low levels of administrative capacity, pervasive corruption among politicians and bureaucratic elites, and an unwillingness of political leaders to share power, or to enforce laws that would maintain order with justice, led to the creation of "soft states" in which governments were unable to organize society for developmental purposes (Myrdal, 1970). Productive assets such as land were generally owned or controlled by a small, privileged elite who opposed reforms that might lead to a greater distribution of income and wealth. Their profits were often invested in the largest urban centers or entirely outside of the country.

Under these conditions entrepreneurship could not easily be promoted and the low levels of income received by the vast majority of people continued to inhibit the expansion of internal demand. With large subsistence populations, it was extremely difficult for governments in developing countries to mobilize savings or generate revenue through direct taxes. Thus, the level of public investment was dependent on revenue raised through indirect taxes, export earnings, foreign aid and external borrowing. As a result, investment remained a small percentage of gross domestic product.

The spread or trickle down effects of growth were constrained by weak market and trade linkages between major industrial centers and rural areas. Many developing nations had "primate city" spatial structures. The bulk of modern economic activities, social services, infrastructure and facilities had been concentrated in the capital city or a single large metropolitan area which dominated the spatial system and economy of the nation (Rondinelli and Ruddle, 1978). Few secondary cities could emerge and large disparities in income and wealth arose between the primary city and the rest of the nation. Disparities between the largest city and the rural hinterlands pulled large numbers of younger, more ambitious and better educated rural people into the metropolitan center and they were followed by less educated and unskilled relatives and friends who often could not find jobs in the city or had access only to the lowest paying employment. Slums and squatter settlements grew quickly in the largest cities of developing nations.

THE LIMITS OF COMPREHENSIVE PLANNING

Perhaps, most importantly, the governments of most poor countries lacked the analytical and administrative capacity to formulate and implement the comprehensive, long-range national development plans required to achieve in a short time what had been attained gradually over a long period in the West. The ability of governments to coordinate their activities among a variety of ministries and agencies to implement a "big push" or leading sector strategy was weak. Few governments could manage public investments effectively let alone guide or control those of the private sector. The experience in Asia is instructive, for national planning and macro-economic development policies did little to promote growth in nearly half of the Asian economies in the 1950s and 1960s, and the progress that was made in four of the "high growth" economies – Hong Kong, Singapore, Taiwan and South Korea – had little to do with long-range national development plans (Rondinelli, 1978).

The failure of national planning to achieve the goals of rapid economic growth and more rational and efficient investment decision-making in Asia can be attributed to two major factors: first, the limited administrative capacity of most Asian governments to implement highly centralized economic plans; and second, unrealistic assumptions and expectations concerning the power of national planning to guide and control national development.

Analysis of plan formulation and implementation in Asia during the 1950s and 1960s reveals a host of recurring and mutually reinforcing administrative problems. Among the most serious were (1) the lack of strong political and administrative support for comprehensive plans; (2) deficiencies in the substantive content of plans that weakened their influence on resource allocation and investment decision-making; (3) the ineffectiveness of macro-planning methods and techniques; (4) weaknesses in government administrative structure and procedures that limited their implementation capacity and their ability to control and evaluate the plan's results.

Weaknesses of political and administrative support

Successful central planning requires political support: the willingness of high-level administrators and officials to make and carry out investment decisions that adhere to the national plan. Yet in most Asian governments strong political and administrative support for comprehensive planning was the exception rather than the rule. The shallowness of support was reflected in opposition by ruling elites to plans suggesting fundamental changes in social and economic structure, the difficulty of planners in establishing their authority or in legitimizing their plans with administrative agencies, the inability to mobilize popular support for major development policies, and the frequent lack of communication between planners and administrators. Indeed, the most crucial decisions regarding social and economic development in Asia were often made outside of the formal planning process.

The lack of strong political and administrative commitment appeared recurringly in evaluations of Asian planning. A "basic problem of development planning in Thailand," one official noted "has been an absence of any keenly felt need for planning" during periods of satisfactory growth. Periods of economic stagnation produced demands for more immediate action than long-range planning could satisfy (Unakul, 1969). Another analyst observed that "planning has never had a glorious day in the Philippines." Not only did it lack strong political support, but also "planning as an attitude of mind, as an institution with all the sense of anticipation, cohesiveness and national discipline that it involves has not been socially accepted." Support was weak throughout the Philippine government structure. "There is no habit for it, no real experience in it," Valdepenas (1973: 265) argued, "and only a lot of attempts at escaping the consistencies and rigors it implies whenever efforts are made to apply it with some seriousness." In Sri Lanka, the political elite who were opposed to rapid social and economic change did little to back national plan priorities. "The absence of strong commitment or even a sense of continuity in development efforts," LaPorte (1970: 167) contended, "has seriously affected public sector activities."

Describing two decades of national planning in Nepal, Rana (1974) noted that few national development decisions were influenced by the National Planning Commission. "The Planning Institution has undergone a series of chameleon-like changes ranging from full executive authority and involvement to a mere advisory role," he contended. "Thus, despite its long history and the four plans it has produced, it is difficult to speak with confidence about its level of institutionalization. Projects whose feasibility the Commission has not analyzed continue to be taken up in the nation's program. The major policies of many sectors are often initiated and financed elsewhere" (Rana, 1974: 660). Cole and Lyman (1971: 217) pointed out that early Korean plans "did little to raise the government's effectiveness." The subsequent acceptance of national planning in Korea seems to have had little to do with increased commitment to comprehensive analysis. Rather the succession to power of a military regime, optimism resulting from rapid economic growth, pressures from international lending agencies, the cohesiveness of Korean society and the close identification of business interests with government development objectives made central controls more tolerable.

Administrators in Thailand not only withheld support, but also often attempted to avoid or subvert national planning procedures, perceiving them not as instruments for promoting economic growth, but as ways "to advance the regime's political interests" (Nophaket, 1973: 205). Thai planners who tried both top-down and bottom-up approaches were constantly frustrated in their attempts to integrate national planning with administrative decision-making. Indeed, the First Plan entirely ignored private investment and dealt summarily with the micro-economic and financial factors of most concern to ministry officials. Ministries and quasi-public corporations often succeeded in avoiding the central planning agency's project review processes by financing investment proposals from operating budgets.

Deficiencies in the content of plans and failure to identify investment projects

In most countries, moreover, the plans themselves lacked substance to guide decision-making and rarely identified specific projects. Most Asian plans stated objectives in vague and amorphous language calculated to gain widespread consensus without specifying implementation strategies, which might have generated conflict and opposition. They often lacked cost estimates and resource allocation proposals; failed to disaggregate macro-economic targets through intermediate sectoral or regional plans and neglected to identify programs and projects for funding in annual or capital budgets. Thus, few plans provided useful guidance for mobilizing and allocating domestic resources or for distributing foreign aid and other external capital to high priority programs.

Despite the claim that national planning would lead to more systematically and comprehensively analyzed decisions, and that central review would provide rationally ordered priorities for the allocation of scarce resources, few national plans actually attained those goals. One evaluator (Lim, 1973: 90–1) of early Malaysian plans noted that

[they] were no more than aggregations of the expansion programmes of separate governmental departments. The planning procedure was simple. Each government department was requested to submit its own claim for recurrent and development expenditure. The total of these claims would normally exceed the funds available and a committee, acting under certain unwritten rules and criteria, would reduce the sum total of the claims until it equalled that of the funds available.

The decisions were made without formally announced priorities and "with no regard for internal consistency." When subsequent attempts were made to correct these deficiencies by adopting quantitative macro-economic models, however, the plans failed to disaggregate, or to predict accurately, investment needs for specific sectors.

National plans have been particularly weak in specifying investment priorities in the private sector, which proved to be the most dynamic part of many Asian economies in the post-war period. In Sri Lanka early plans paid "very little attention . . . to initiating, formulating and assisting investment in the private sector" (Karunatilake, 1971: 270). There was virtually no relationship between private investment decisions and national plan recommendations in Nepal in the late 1960s. "None of the industries for which targets had been provided by the Third Plan fulfilled their targets," one critic (Rana, 1974: 50) pointed out. "In fact, more than half of them were not even under production in 1970." Other industries succeeded beyond expectations, even though the plan set no targets for them. "In fact, success, where it was achieved, was either due to foreign aid negotiation totally independent of the plan, or was, in the case of stainless steel and nylon yarn, ad hoc decisions in complete contradiction of plan aims."

Evaluations also revealed the weaknesses of national planning in linking development recommendations to public budget decisions. Reviewing planning in Thailand during the 1960s, one official argued that "no consistency check was attempted for the plan nor were criteria laid down for selection of projects, including cost-benefit analysis" (Marzouk, 1972: 431). Another observer (Unakul, 1969: 68) contended that

> Apart from the formation of sectoral programs, estimates were made for the production of major commodities at the end of the plan period. However, the final "target" of five percent growth of GNP was more a forecast than a target. Besides the government was not in a position to ensure that the entire program set out would actually be implemented. Besides, a considerable shortcoming in expenditure resulted. Nevertheless, the five percent "target" was achieved, even though it was largely due to the remarkable performance of the private sector, for which the plan had little to say.

Budget decisions in the Philippines rarely had any relationship to plan priorities and recommendations. Indeed, budget decision-making was often totally divorced from national planning. Budgets were worked out incrementally, through bargaining and negotiation on the basis of immediate political and administrative criteria. Although the Budget Commission was supposed to be guided by the National Economic Council's (NEC) plans, they were not always endorsed by the President. The Budget Commission instead prepared annual expenditure authorizations on the basis of needs submitted by operating departments. Appropriations were then either cut or increased during reviews by the President's staff and again during Congressional consideration, usually without reference to comprehensive development plans. Moreover, the Central Bank set monetary, credit and foreign exchange policies independently of both the NEC and other planning agencies (UNDP, 1972). In Ceylon, the national plan served primarily as a statement of government policy, but outlined broad economic and social strategies in such sweeping language that, as one Ceylon official (Karunatilake, 1971: 268) noted, "the planning techniques adopted were not having a significant impact on growth."

And even where attempts have been made to focus on specific invest-ment implications, as did Indonesia's plans of the early 1960s, political goals often dominated and biased the decisions. Indonesia's initial plans, seeking to create national political solidarity, "grossly under-represented the financial costs and the economic sacrifices necessary" for implementation, even after control securely passed from the colonial to the national government (Schulz, 1972: 62). In Nepal government officials complained of the "lack of relationship between the budget . . . and the Five-Year Plan" (Rana, 1974: 51). Caiden and Wildavsky (1974: 251), reviewing the effect of planning on budgeting in a number of developing countries, concluded that "the annual budget rarely does what the plan intends." They found large discrepancies between planned investment and amounts actually budgeted. Singapore either exceeded or fell short of planned investments in each sector. Malaysian investments in infrastructure and utilities outstripped targetted allo-cations during the first three national plans, and investment in social services and agriculture, which received the highest priorities, failed to reach projected levels.

Ineffectiveness of central planning methods and techniques

The very techniques of planning often rendered national economic plans inoperable. Evaluations of Asian planning suggest a number of problems.

Models and techniques developed in Western industrialized countries were often uncritically applied in Asia. The macro-economic models used in Malaysia's national development plans were found to be both inappropriate and inaccurate for forecasting national economic trends. Criticizing the use of an aggregate Harrod–Domar model, one Malaysian economist (Lim, 1973: 121) pointed out that "even if the model were representative of the structural conditions of Malaysia, its usefulness would be reduced considerably by the shortage of reliable statistical data." The model's fundamental assumption, that the shortage of capital was a crucial bottleneck to growth, did not apply in Malaysia. The data required to calculate the incremental capital-output ratio (ICOR), on which the model was based, had to be approximated using arbitrary − and what later proved to be inaccurate − assumptions.

A leading Thai planner (Unakul, 1969: 74) noted the limitations of quantitative analysis under conditions found in most Asian countries, where "available data are neither comprehensive, reliable nor timely." One evaluator of Thailand's national plans for the 1960s claimed that not only were the macro-economic models based on highly simplified economic assumptions, but also the World Bank Consultative Committee prepared the quantitative forecasts "basically by intuition." Marzouk (1972: 437) pointed out that rough guesses had to be made to estimate GDP by expenditure type because of the paucity of data." And the director of NEDB's Economic and Social Planning Division (Unakul, 1969: 70) noted that private sector investment and consumption had to be considered as residuals by making the assumption that production of and demand for goods and services would remain in equilibrium through the end of the 1960s. That procedure, he contended, led planners "to assume away the central problem of planning; namely, how to adjust the resources and expenditures in both the public and private sectors to meet the objectives of growth and stability."

Inadequate administrative capacity for central planning and control

Finally, coordination of administrative decisions concerning the allocation and investment of national resources must be an essential element of national planning if it is to achieve its targets and goals. Unless administrative agencies, quasi-public corporations and private investors are willing to cooperate with the central planning agency in carrying out planned activities and to coordinate with each other in implementing programs and projects, central planning is meaningless. Yet, in reality, plan implementation in Asia has always been severely limited by inadequate administrative structures and coordinative procedures for guiding or controlling investment decisions.

In part, the problem was due to the substantive deficiencies in the content of plans noted earlier – their failure to specify investment needs and to anticipate administrative requirements for implementation. Rana (1974: 23) complained that the effectiveness of planning in Nepal was severely limited by the failure of planners to analyze the administrative and political implications of their proposals. Concern with macro-economic analysis and quantitative forecasting, along with the application of Western development theories, blinded them to the weaknesses of indigenous administrative capability. Arguing that the low level of managerial capacity was the most crucial obstacle to development in Nepal, Rana concluded that "management, organization and enterprise are matters not precisely quantifiable and it is perhaps not surprising that westerners, and westerners highly specialized in economics, looking at our countries should have tended to take these factors for granted."

But it is precisely these organizational and administrative factors that appeared repeatedly in evaluations of national planning as major constraints on implementation. In Sri Lanka during the 1950s and 1960s economic achievements always fell behind planned targets; decisions regularly departed from government guidelines. "More emphasis seems to have been devoted to the preparation of elaborate paper documents," Karunatilake (1971: 263) complained, "rather than to the project content of the plan and how best it could be implemented to produce quick results." And even after 1965, when the government explicitly admitted that national planning had little influence on essential development decisions and disaggregated planning by sector, progress was still limited by administrative constraints. Neither the Department of National Planning nor the ministries had the management procedures or technically qualified manpower needed to prepare and implement sectoral programs. After a decade of comprehensive planning, they discovered that even within the national planning agency very few officials had the experience necessary to determine balance of payments effects or gross domestic product implications of sectoral plans.

To the extent that national planning required cooperation among ministries and with the central planning agencies, or depended on the ability of a central agency to coordinate, monitor and evaluate resource allocations and investments, it was rarely successful in Asia. A Pakistani planning official (Hussain, 1973: 458) reported that a major obstacle to executing that country's bottom-up process "is the total absence of co-ordination among various departmental agencies during implementation of projects." In Thailand the Budget Bureau made fiscal and financial policies using its own criteria, leaving the national planning agency uninformed of its intentions. Despite formal requirements that it cooperate, the Budget Bureau did not usually provide revenue and expenditure information necessary for coordination between planners and budget officials (Unakul, 1969: 72).

Difficulties in implementing national plans also arose from the inability of the central government to evaluate, monitor and control the decisions of administrative agencies. Even when planning and administrative structures were reorganized for that purpose, the results were disappointing. Thailand's requirement, that each operating ministry and government agency submit quarterly evaluation and review reports, quickly inundated planning and budgeting officials with more information than they could possibly analyze, or that the Inspector General could investigate even if the planners were able to find discrepancies between plans and operations. Indeed, Changrien (1970: 24) noted that administrative reorganization of monitoring functions did little to improve coordination even among the review agencies:

> There is hardly any coordination between the Bureau of Planning and Research, the Budget Bureau and NEDB in this supervision and coordination work although all of them are in the Prime Minister's Office. The net result of this lack of coordination and ineffectiveness of the reporting system is that the Government Performance Information Centre has almost ceased to be operative and the back-log of reports . . . in the Bureau of Planning and Research continues to mount. Supervision cannot be exercised over the government operations effectively and coordination is often left to chance.

In Malaysia the government established "operations rooms" in an effort to evaluate and supervise plan implementation. They were effective only as long as the Prime Minister placed political pressure on the bureaucracy to report progress and coordinate activities. But the system itself was quickly bureaucratized. As political pressure from the Prime Minister eased, the system faltered (Esman, 1972).

In brief, the failure of comprehensive national planning, either to achieve a clear record of success in promoting economic growth or to guide and control resource allocation and investment decisions, prompted the search in the 1960s for more effective policy-making instruments. The dismal record of national planning in the Third World led to a fundamental reappraisal of both macro-economic development objectives and planning procedures.

ECONOMIC GROWTH THROUGH SOCIAL CHANGE: OVERCOMING OBSTACLES TO DEVELOPMENT

Capital intensive industrialization strategies of the 1950s did not only fail to produce rapid and sustained growth in developing countries, but in many they also created "dual economies" and reinforced a cycle of poverty that became more difficult to break. The foreign aid strategies of the 1950s strengthened the forces perpetuating poverty in developing nations, and by the end of the decade came under attack by both liberal and conservative economists in the United States. Milton Friedman (1958) for instance, while supporting the concept of foreign aid, questioned the three major assumptions underlying capital-intensive industrialization policies. He challenged the propositions that availability of capital was the key to economic development, that underdeveloped countries were unable to mobilize capital internally, and that centralized, comprehensive macro-economic planning was a prerequisite to development. "All three propositions are at best misleading half-truths," Friedman argued. He noted that developing nations had been mobilizing capital and other resources for high priority investments for centuries. But, he insisted, other conditions were more important for promoting economic development, and these had to be created before capital could be used effectively. Moreover, Friedman (1958: 256) argued that the prescriptions for macro-economic development planning were unlikely to be useful or appropriate in developing nations. "Such a centralized program is likely to be a hindrance, not a help," he maintained.

Economic development is a process of changing old ways of doing things, of venturing into the unknown. It requires a maximum of flexibility, of possibility for experimentation. No one can predict in advance what will turn out to be the most effective use of a nation's productive resources. Yet the essence of a program of economic development is that it introduces rigidity and inflexibility.

Others insisted that bilateral foreign assistance that was tied to procurement in the donor country prevented governments from using the funds for high priority needs and for non-industrial purposes. The conditions under which aid was given often precluded its use for investments other than show-piece projects and high technology production. Ultimately these capital transfers discouraged indigenous savings and internal capital formation in developing nations. The benefits of aid often went to a small elite in power who were unwilling to undertake social and economic reforms or to initiate programs that would overcome the obstacles to economic expansion and diversification. Griffin and Enos (1970: 325) reflecting on similar conclusions arrived at by World Bank officials at the end of the 1950s, claimed that "foreign aid tends to strengthen the status quo, it enables those in power to evade and avoid fundamental reforms; it does little more than patch plaster on the deteriorating social edifice."

International assistance agencies began to target their technical and financial assistance during the 1960s more carefully on specific problems and conditions in developing countries that were thought to be obstacles or bottlenecks to industrial expansion and economic growth. An underlying assumption of these new approaches, which had been evolving over a number of years, was that social changes had to precede economic expansion because adverse conditions in developing nations were obstacles to growth. Greater attention had to be given to programs for asset redistribution, institution-building, population and family planning, labor-intensive and small-scale industrialization, agricultural expansion and human resources development. Insistence on the formulation of comprehensive long-range master plans gave way to sectoral programming and increased attention to project formulation and design. Again, both liberal and conservative economists hailed flexibility as an essential element of development planning. Friedman (1958: 256), for instance, argued for development policies that would create an economic and political environment more conducive to widespread participation in economic activities:

What is required in the underdeveloped countries is the release of the energies of millions of able, active, and vigorous people who have been chained by ignorance, custom, and tradition. Such people exist in every underdeveloped country. If it seems otherwise, it is because we tend to seek them in our own image in "big business" on the Western model rather than in the villages and farms and in the shops and bazaars that line the streets of the crowded cities in many a poor country. These people require only a favorable environment to transform the face of their countries.

Others insisted that development programs would have to be strongly guided by national governments and international assistance agencies through sectoral planning and investment programming. Internal resources and foreign aid would have to be chaneled into sectors where bottlenecks were greatest and into programs that would generate fundamental social changes.

Focus on key sectors

Development theories that evolved during the 1960s began to focus on the search for the key sectors into which national resources and international assistance should be channeled. Some economists, such as Schultz (1964) saw agricultural development as the new "engine of growth" in poor countries. Johnston and Mellor (1961) insisted that agricultural sector development would have a number of beneficial effects. It would increase food supplies needed to meet the nutritional requirements of the population in poor countries and maintain lower food prices as demand increased. Expansion of agricultural exports would provide higher incomes to farmers and peasants and increase foreign exchange earnings. Higher agricultural productivity would free surplus labor for industrial employment and generate capital that could be invested in manufacturing and industrial sectors to absorb the surplus labor. Increased income for rural people would create larger demand for both agricultural and industrial products.

But the semi-targetted aid strategies of the 1960s were based on more than a leading sector investment theory. It was widely recognized that the linkages among sectors had to be created in developing nations and that aid had to be channeled into a variety of supporting activities as well as into sectoral production. Thus, aid agencies provided technical and financial assistance for research into new high-yielding seed varieties, irrigation system construction, improvement of agricultural training and extension programs, the creation of marketing systems, the organization of cooperatives and farmers' associations and the initiation of agricultural credit schemes.

It also became clear during the 1960s that social, economic and political problems were inextricably related. The existence of some conditions had to precede the creation of others and among the most important was the redistribution of productive assets. Some development theorists argued that breaking up the monopoly of land ownership was the most effective way of redistributing assets to the poor and making income distribution more equitable. The redistribution of lands owned by plantations and family estates to cultivators and peasants would reduce rents and increase income in rural areas while putting more land into cultivation (Warriner, 1964). The US aid program not only funded many of the land reform programs in developing countries, but also sent technical experts to help carry them out. United Nations agencies urged governments to adopt land redistribution policies.

The low levels of administrative capacity in governments of developing nations also prompted international aid agencies to provide technical assistance in public administration. Public administration specialists sought to reorganize bureaucracies in developing nations, establish civil service systems based on merit and skill, improve personnel administration, establish public enterprises and reform the budgeting and investment allocation procedures in Third World countries. Emphasis was placed on "institution-building" as a means of modernizing governments and of expanding their capacities to carry out development activities more effectively.

High rates of population growth were also seen as fundamental obstacles to economic and social progress in developing nations during the 1960s. Thus large amounts of aid went to private and voluntary organizations promoting population control and family planning. Aid was also channeled into human resources development. Assistance organizations worked with governments to establish formal, informal and vocational education systems in developing countries. Harbison (1962: 3), among others, argued that human resources development "is concerned with the two-fold objective of building skills and providing productive employment for unutilized and underutilized manpower." Aid programs would be used to increase the supply of professionals and scientists in developing countries, prepare young people to take up technical positions for which para-professional training was needed and relieve the severe shortages of managerial and administrative personnel in the public and private sectors. Of high priority was expanding the numbers of trained teachers, the shortage of which Harbison called the "master bottleneck" that constrained the entire process of human development. Educational systems would also have to be reorganized to train people for occupational roles as craftsmen, clerical workers, and entrepreneurs. Large amounts of aid were also provided to send talented government officials and managers to the United States, Britain and some European countries for graduate and professional degrees and for short-term professional and technical training. School systems within poor countries were reorganized to reflect American, British or French standards and educational objectives.

The International Labor Office (ILO), concluding that unemployment had become "chronic and intractable" in most developing nations during the late 1950s and early 1960s, focused its attention on promoting labor-intensive, employment-generating industrialization, agro-industries, small-scale manufacturing and informal sector enterprises that would absorb labor surpluses in the Third World.

Sectoral planning and systematic project design

The shift from untargetted to semi-targetted aid was reflected not only in the sectoral development policies adopted by international assistance organizations during the 1960s, but also in their planning and implementation procedures. Both bilateral and multinational assistance agencies abandoned requirements for national, long-range, macroeconomic development plans and turned instead to sectoral planning and investment programming. They also began to give greater emphasis to project preparation and design. The shifts came as the result of the growing acceptance of two basic assumptions in international assistance agencies that were made explicit by World Bank official Albert Waterston (1965). The first was that assistance would have little impact unless it was more precisely tailored to the needs of developing countries and aimed more effectively at overcoming specific problems or obstacles to development through well-conceived and efficiently organized development projects. National development plans had failed to disaggregate goals and objectives into programs of investment and provide guidance about the priority and selection of projects. At the same time, officials of international aid agencies assumed that governments in developing countries did not have the administrative capacity to use foreign aid effectively. Waterston (1971: 240) maintained that "technical ministries, departments and aid agencies in most countries do not have the staffs qualified to (a) identify, evaluate and prepare good projects, (b) fix project priorities in accordance with well devised time tables, and (c) operate completed projects efficiently." But officials in international agencies also believed that individual projects and programs would not lead to coherent and well-focused development strategies and that aid had to be channeled into specific sectors in a highly coordinated fashion. Thus, the World Bank's annual report for 1967 pointed out that "an approach being increasingly employed in the developing countries is to undertake an analysis of a particular sector of an economy with a view to preparing a coordinated investment program for that sector and to selecting priority projects within it" (World Bank, 1967: 16).

Aid strategies were to be formulated and implemented during the 1960s through two seemingly contradictory approaches. On one hand the World Bank and USAID experimented with program and sectoral lending arrangements that granted developing nations much more flexibility in using aid in priority sectors. These funding agreements did not tie aid to conventional project formats. On the other hand all international assistance organizations adopted more complex and rigid requirements and procedures for identifying, preparing, appraising and implementing projects.

The US Agency for International Development began making sectoral and program loans in the early 1960s to a limited number of countries, mostly in Latin America, to finance imports for coordinated investment programs. Program loans were based on self-help agreements between USAID and the recipient government in which the borrower pledged to make detailed sectoral analyses, establish specific and precise goals for development of the sector and outline proposals for policies, programs and projects to be supported with foreign aid. The Latin America Bureau in USAID made the most extensive use of sectoral loans because officials were dissatisfied with the macro-economic approaches to development assistance employed during the 1950s and with the rigidities of the project format. Latin America Bureau officials insisted that standard prescriptions for development and inflexible procedures for aid administration would inhibit social and economic change in developing nations (USAID, 1972a). Between 1967 and 1972 USAID authorized twenty-one sector loans totalling more than $438 million, which were used primarily for agricultural development, land reform, employment generation, education and municipal and urban development. Income redistribution was an explicit objective of many of the sectoral plans (USAID, 1972b).

At the same time, international assistance organizations were adopting more complex and systematic procedures for planning and implementing development projects. Attempting to overcome deficiencies in planning and administrative capacity in less developed nations, aid agencies took a more active and direct role in project identification, preparation, design and analysis. They formulated a complex set of procedures for testing preinvestment feasibility. To varying degrees the World Bank, USAID and the UN Specialized Agencies insisted on quantitative justifications of project proposals, including extensive market and needs analyses, technical feasibility studies, economic cost-benefit calculations or precise estimates of internal rate of return, and studies of administrative and managerial capacity to implement proposed projects. Preparation and selection guidelines were designed to ensure that proposals were compatible with lending institution policies and priorities (Rondinelli, 1976).

World Bank officials insisted, for instance, that effective implementation of development projects was influenced strongly by detailed preparation and appraisal procedures. "Careful project preparation in advance of expenditure is," Gittinger (1972: 1) would later contend, "if not absolutely essential, at least the best available means to ensure efficient economic use of capital funds and to increase the chances of on-schedule implementation." Bank officials began investing substantial amounts of money in detailed feasibility analyses and project appraisals, insisting on thorough exploration of the "creditworthiness" of borrowing countries and of the bankability of project proposals. They believed that the more elaborate and detailed the feasibility and appraisal analyses, the greater the probability that the projects would be implemented successfully.

But others argued that preparatory analyses were not sufficient to ensure successful implementation. More systematic and detailed management procedures were needed after a project was approved. Thus, a number of techniques were adopted from the fields of management science, operations research and corporate planning that had been used by private firms and defense agencies in the United States and Britain to guide the management of development projects. Techniques that applied mathematical logic to organizational performance, cost-effectiveness analyses, precise time phasing of project activities, and control of operations through the use of computers and complex reporting requirements were all prescribed by management consultants within international assistance agencies. Linear programming, CPM-PERT

scheduling and control techniques and mathematical models for predict-
ing economic and social behavior in developing countries all became
fashionable in managing development projects.

Re-evaluation of aid impacts and procedures

Although the new international development policies and aid strategies
were more successful in disaggregating and focusing aid on critical problems the overall results in developing nations had been disappointing.
Progress was made in most countries in lowering the rate of population
growth; a few countries such as Taiwan, Malaysia, Brazil and South
Korea were achieving high rates of economic growth; agricultural production increased in many developing nations; and health conditions
improved for higher and middle income groups in the developing world.
Yet land reform failed in more nations than it succeeded. Population
growth still outpaced agricultural and industrial production in most poor
countries. High levels of illiteracy, poverty, child death, and malnutrition were common in Third World nations. Evaluations of the UN's
First Development Decade found that progress had been slow and
halting during the 1960s and that the poor in most developing nations
were no better off at the end of the decade than they had been at the beginning. Few nations had attained the levels of economic growth projected
in their national development plans. A study undertaken for the World
Bank (Pearson, 1969) found that despite overall increases in economic
growth in developing nations during the 1960s, in 1967 nearly 70 percent
of the population (outside of mainland China) lived in countries where
per capita income grew at less than 2 percent a year and where population
growth rates generally exceeded increases in national output.

By the end of the 1960s international evaluation commissions became
increasingly critical of the ability of assistance organizations to deliver
aid effectively and to break the bottlenecks and overcome the obstacles to
development. The Pearson Commission (Pearson, 1969) reviewed the
entire aid system for the World Bank and found that if technical and
financial assistance was to become more effective it would have to be dis-
associated from political and military objectives of the aid-givers, untied
from procurement requirements, and channeled more flexibly through
multilateral organizations. The Commission saw the increasingly rigid
and formal bureaucratic procedures surrounding international assistance
as a hindrance to its effective use in developing nations. It noted (Pearson, 1969: 169) that developing nations often lacked adequate policies
for using aid, "leading to duplication of requests and confusion among
government ministries interested in furthering their own interests."

An examination of the United Nations' system of technical assistance by the Jackson (1969) Committee came to similar conclusions. Among the Jackson Committee's most severe criticisms was that foreign aid was not tailored to the needs of developing countries. Western practices and institutions – or solutions to problems in one developing nation – were often transferred to Third World countries without modification. "Instead of measuring and cutting the cloth on the spot in accordance with individual circumstances and wants," the Committee (Jackson, 1969: 171) claimed, "a ready-made garment is produced and forced to fit afterwards."

But one of the largest stumbling blocks to the use of aid in promoting national development, the Pearson Commission (Pearson, 1969: 29) pointed out, was the failure of governments in most developing nations to take action that would distribute income and productive assets more equitably. "They have only recently begun to recognize that measures to make income distribution more equitable not only serve a social objective," the Commission argued, "but also are necessary for a sustained development effort."

ECONOMIC GROWTH WITH SOCIAL EQUITY: CHANNELING ASSISTANCE TO THE POOR MAJORITY

Analyses done during the early 1970s of the performance of developing economies over the previous quarter of a century reinforced emerging arguments that aid must be channeled more directly to the poorest groups in developing societies if they are to benefit from and contribute to economic development.

In a review for the World Bank of the trends in economic development from 1950 to 1975, Morawetz (1977) found that the growth that occurred was very unevenly distributed among developing nations and that statistics indicating overall progress in Third World countries often masked serious disparities. Although the average annual growth rate in GNP for eighty developing nations had been a respectable 3.4 percent, a rate that exceeded the growth rates of GNP in the industrialized countries (3.2 percent a year), performance in individual developing nations varied widely. The developing countries' average had been raised by high rates of growth in GNP in oil rich Middle Eastern countries (5.2 percent) and by rapid industrialization in a few of the East Asian economies (3.9 percent). But African and Latin American nations had increased their GNP by an average of only 2.5 percent a year and Southeast Asian economies had grown at an average rate of only 1.7 percent a year. Many of the poorest countries were completely bypassed by economic progress. Honduras, Chile, Ghana and Bolivia, for instance, hardly increased their economic output at all (less than 1 percent a year in the 1960s and early 1970s) and others such as Bangladesh, Rwanda and Upper Volta registered negative growth rates.

Thus, statistics that showed substantial progress in economic development blurred the fact that disparities between rich and poor countries had actually increased over twenty-five years. Although growth rates remained stable for the eighty countries analyzed by Morawetz (1977), absolute disparities between industrialized and developing nations in per capita GNP increased threefold. Average GNP per capita in industrialized nations was $2000 greater than that in developing nations in 1950, but by 1975 the differences more than doubled to nearly $5000. Even the fastest growing economies during the late 1960s and early 1970s, such as Korea and Taiwan, were unable to reduce the gap substantially. Differences in per capita GNP between these nations and the developed countries doubled during the quarter century since 1950. By the early 1970s there remained at least thirty-seven countries with a combined population of over 1.2 billion that had per capita GNP levels of less than $300 a year, and another fifteen countries with an additional 270 million people with per capita GNP of less than $500. Nearly three-quarters of the population in less developed nations lived in relative or absolute poverty (income equivalents of less than $75 and $50 a year respectively). Less than half of the population in the thirty-seven least developed nations was literate. Average annual population increases in these countries were more than double those in developed countries; life expectancy averaged less than fifty years, and child death rates were eighteen times higher on average than in industrialized countries (World Bank, 1979).

Moreover, it became increasingly apparent during the late 1960s and early 1970s that the number of people living in dire poverty in developing nations was increasing rather than diminishing. The conditions of many living at or near subsistence levels had been progressively worsening rather than improving. It was also recognized more widely among economists, development theorists and aid officials that high rates of economic growth – with all of the inherent constraints on spread effects and trickling down – would not ameliorate poverty in most developing countries. In all but a few nations that had achieved high rates of economic growth the conditions of the poor grew worse rather than better. Studies done in the late 1960s and early 1970s indicated that the spread effects from sectoral development policies were as sluggish as those produced by macro-economic strategies. In a study of forty-three developing nations, Adelman and Morris (1973) found that in all but the very rich and the poorest nations, income distributions became more skewed as their economies grew. In many of the developing nations that they analyzed the highest income groups (the top 20 percent of the population) received more than 65 percent of the income and the lowest 40 percent of the population received as low as 10 percent of the nation's income. They found a good deal of evidence that questioned the validity of the Kuznets curve concept. Adelman and Morris (1967) found that in many developing nations the richest groups had indeed benefited from initial economic growth, but that even after the economy broke out of extreme dualism, the benefits went mainly to middle-income groups, with little or nothing trickling down to the poorest. The position of the poorest 40 percent of the population worsened both relatively and absolutely.

The accumulating evidence suggested that equitable and sustained economic growth required the creation of an extensive base of participation in productive activities in developing nations by including vast numbers of people living at or near subsistence levels through what Adelman called a "human-resource-intensive development strategy." In a study for the World Bank, Chenery (1974) also found that the vast majority of the poor had been excluded from the benefits of economic growth "by a number of specific disabilities that can be summed up as the lack of physical and human capital and lack of access." These disabilities could be overcome, he noted, only by designing policies to assure equitable distribution of income and that took account of the specific social and economic characteristics of the poor. Adelman argued that few, if any, single sector development policies, in isolation, would have a real impact on reaching the poorest groups in developing societies. Those nations that had achieved growth with relative equity had certain characteristics in common that provided clues to the kinds of policies that might have a beneficial effect. They had political leaders who were strongly committed to economic development based on broad participation in economic activities; they received massive amounts of foreign assistance that allowed them to tackle a wide variety of social and economic problems in combination; they instituted and successfully carried out strong programs of asset redistribution prior to the period in which economic growth was most rapid that allowed for widespread sharing in the benefits of growth; and they placed a great deal of emphasis on human resources development in the pre-growth period. From these lessons, Adelman (1975) and others concluded that "asset redistribution and the redistribution of opportunities for access to asset accumulation are a necessary first step for the initiation of equitable growth." But, they also argued that growth and equitable distribution policies could not be separated. In countries where sluggish growth followed asset redistribution, the value of redistributed assets declined leaving the poor no better off, while the richest 20 percent of the population captured windfall profits (Adelman 1975: 70).

Others began questioning more seriously the value of detailed and complex planning procedures and management controls that international assistance agencies and planning ministries in many developing nations had been applying to the formulation and implementation of development projects.

As their own supervision, monitoring and evaluation reports began to indicate, international assistance agencies created a system for project administration during the 1960s and 1970s that was beyond their capacity and that of developing nations to implement. The tendency to abstract, rationalize, standardize, control, and complicate not only created conditions for its own failures but also inflicted hardships and frustrations on those the system was designed to benefit. Observing this trend toward more sophisticated analysis and detailed planning for rural development projects in Africa, Chambers and Belshaw (1973: 6.3) concluded that "together these lead away from reality, from what is feasible, and the cumulative increments of change which can gradually transform performance, and encourage the design and propagation of ideal models which are not only unattainable but also liable to impair rather than improve performance." Assessing the impact of increasingly complex procedures on project administration, they argued that "the perfectionist planner and the intellectual academic are both susceptible to recommending yet more planning, more detailed and specific statement of objectives, the generation and analysis of more data, the identification, elaboration, and choice between more alternatives." The trend toward more complex analysis, they concluded, had two unfortunate results: "generating an insatiable appetite for planners, who are far from costless; and reducing the chances of anything happening on the ground."

To many officials in developing countries adoption of foreign procedures and administrative reforms served no rational purpose other than to obtain external funds. Complex appraisal and management procedures could often be applied only by foreign experts, academics and consultants, with no guarantee that the analyses would beneficially alter the substance of a proposal, that the project would be more palatable to local bureaucrats or politicians, or that the projects would be better implemented within a traditional organizational and political structure. Many of the prescriptions were simply irrelevant to the conditions under which government officials had to operate. Or worse, they conflicted with internal political processes required to obtain support and approval for project proposals.

Obstacles to systematic project planning and implementation, as will be seen later in this book, pervaded bureaucracies in developing nations. Unless high-level political support protected a proposal through early stages, rivalries, conflicts and bureaucratic competition delayed or killed even "high-priority" projects justified by voluminous feasibility studies. Politicians in strategic positions within central ministries or provincial governments often pushed through pet projects that were badly formulated and lacking feasibility studies, displacing those delayed by intensive analysis and appraisal. Told by international experts to define goals and objectives clearly, government officials knew that it was frequently to their own advantage to keep objectives and purposes "fuzzy" and amorphous, to avoid unequivocally stating intended accomplishments, and to resist losing flexibility by submitting detailed designs and operating plans. In an atmosphere of uncertainty and resistance to change, success depended on obtaining and preserving a strong coalition of political support. Projects survived by attracting advocates with different goals, purposes and expectations, each seeking different outputs and "payoffs." Objectives were better left vague, allowing each reviewer to form his own conclusions, than made explicit at the risk of generating conflict and opposition or of losing flexibility during implementation.

While macro-economists, planners and management analysts in international assistance agencies devised objective and rational allocation and appraisal techniques, sophisticated selection procedures and systematic scheduling and control devices in search of optimal resource allocation and utilization within the national economy, government officials were concerned with political compromises and tradeoffs necessary to push any project – optimal or not – through a politically influenced selection and execution process. And even if a project's sponsors wanted to define objectives precisely and clearly relate them to national development policies, problems arose. Goals, targets and priorities were kept vague in project proposals for the same reason that objectives of national development plans had been ill-defined: to obtain consensus and minimize political conflict. Goals changed quickly in developing nations; policies were displaced by succeeding regimes. Those developed for external consumption often had low internal priority, and those espoused by ministry heads were often publicly acknowledged by national political leaders but given little budgetary support.

But even if agreement on goals, priorities and desired results existed, developing nations often lacked reliable statistics, adequate data and skilled analysts to apply the procedures prescribed by international funding institutions. A USAID education sector analysis team sent to Brazil, for example, found it nearly impossible to apply the prescribed methods in one of the more economically advanced developing countries. Neither the education ministry nor the state governments had the data or trained manpower to apply sophisticated analytical techniques. The mission (USAID, 1970: 6) reported that:

> The pattern of financing of education in Brazil makes it difficult to effectively analyze the cost efficiency of the education sector or the precise future financial needs of the system. It is very difficult to satisfactorily plan the expansion of education programs or to know to what extent the effort to increase productivity of existing resources might have a significant impact on decreasing per pupil costs. Likewise it is impossible to evaluate the cost-benefits of investments in innovations of educational technology if costs of present educational methods are not known.

Perhaps the ultimate irony was that many developing countries had been judged backward, inefficient and defective in administrative capacity because they could not apply analytical and management techniques, the efficacy and practicality of which remained unproven even in advanced industrialized nations. By the early 1970s a number of studies were emerging in the United States that questioned the usefulness of systems analysis, quantitative models and planning-programing-budgeting schemes in public decision-making (Wildavsky, 1969; Schick, 1973; Hoos, 1972). Studies of weapons systems projects in the United States, from which many of the planning and management procedures had been borrowed, indicated that PERT and other scheduling and control techniques gave a "myth of managerial effectiveness" to project administration without contributing to substantive results (Sapolski, 1972). An extensive analysis of factors determining project success commissioned by the US National Aeronautical and Space Administration (Murphy et al., 1974: 9) found that "creation of elaborate and detailed reporting and control systems . . . detracts from success by causing excessive delays, red-tape, superficial reports and inadequate information flows."

Thus, by the late 1960s both strategies of economic development and procedures and techniques of project planning and implementation came under increasing scrutiny.

NEW DIRECTIONS IN DEVELOPMENT ASSISTANCE

The changes that came about in international assistance strategy during the early 1970s were the result of a confluence of forces. For nearly a decade the purposes of and approaches to foreign assistance had been re-evaluated, as had the directions and objectives of development policy. A steady process of learning by scholars, practitioners and policy-makers in both industrialized and developing nations brought many conventional assumptions of development theory into question, as had the frequent attacks on mainstream economic theories by radical and socialist thinkers. Although socialism and radical Marxism, which reject main-stream economics, influenced development theory quite significantly, international assistance organizations did not embrace the more radical approaches embodied in dependency theory and revolutionary political ideology. The rationale for "targeting" benefits to constituent groups of the poor, however, reflected the influence of social scientists who were more concerned with the nature, direction and implications of social change than simply with the level or pace of economic growth, and of many economists who were critical of the conventional approaches used to aid developing nations during the 1950s and 1960s.

An earlier belief prevalent among development economists that economic growth and equitable distribution of income were conflicting goals was largely displaced during the 1970s by evidence that deliberate efforts to distribute income and wealth more equitably in countries such as Taiwan, South Korea and Malaysia did not impair high levels of economic growth and, in fact, created a broader base of participation in economic activities that reinforced and accelerated growth processes. It was also more widely recognized that "automatic" mechanisms rarely produce the expected spread and filtering effects in poor countries and that policies must be deliberately designed to incorporate peripheral areas and marginal groups into the economy if poverty is to be ameliorated.

Moreover, political leaders and scholars from developing nations had begun asserting their own interests and views in international forums. The steadily growing realization that problems in developing nations differed drastically from those faced by industrialized nations brought about a fundamental rethinking of development policy that led to new, more pragmatic, approaches to international assistance in the early 1970s. They were clearly reflected in the US Foreign Assistance Act passed by Congress in 1973.

The Foreign Assistance Act, as noted in chapter 1, shifted the focus of American aid from a program that had attempted to build economies in developing countries in the Western image to one that would assist developing nations to follow their own paths to development. The new aid program would give less emphasis to maximizing growth through macro-economic policies and pursue what the House of Representatives'

Foreign Affairs Committee called a "people-oriented problem solving form of assistance." It put aside the capital transfer approach in favor of using a wide variety of technical and financial instruments for solving social and economic problems. The previous emphasis in aid strategy on maximizing economic growth was tempered by a concern for dealing with basic human problems that kept the vast majority of the population in Third World countries in poverty. For the first time international assistance agencies were to take into account the characteristics and needs of the poor as the major beneficiaries of aid programs.

The arguments made for these new directions in development assistance were based on familiar humanitarian and political motives. The Foreign Affairs Committee of the US Congress pointed out that the economic, political and military security of the United States depended in part on the progress of nations in which large numbers of people lived in poverty and deprivation. Aid was a means of influencing developing country governments to follow policies that were consistent with American foreign policy. The humanitarian appeal also continued to be strong. The House Foreign Affairs Committee noted in its report on the Foreign Assistance Act of 1973 that "we Americans annually spend six times what we allot for foreign assistance on cigarettes and other tobacco products. We spend three times as much for toys and sports supplies; three times as much for toilet articles and perfumes. Surely, our consumption oriented society can spare something for fellow human beings who have virtually nothing." (*US Code Congressional and Administrative News*, 1973: 2811).

But above all, the changing strategies reflected a somewhat more sophisticated understanding of the dynamics of development, the constraints on economic and social change in developing nations and the political and social forces that influence the processes of change in Third World countries. Although these strategies identified the poorest groups in developing nations as the primary beneficiaries of aid, the new policies were not conceived of, or intended to be, welfare programs. In its report accompanying the Foreign Assistance Act of 1973, the Foreign Affairs Committee argued that "we are learning that if the poorest majority can participate in development by having productive work and access to basic education, health care and adequate diets, then increased economic growth and social justice can go hand in hand." The president of the Overseas Development Council (Grant, 1973: 65) insisted that "greater equality of opportunity to participate, rather than more aid of the welfare variety, is the most urgent need of the poor within countries (and of the low income states within the community of nations)." He noted that "this equity can be more efficient than inequity and 'trickle down' in advancing growth in both rich and poor countries."

The new development assistance policies also recognized that economic growth and equitable distribution of income were not incompatible. An analyst (Paolillo, 1976: 5) for the Foreign Affairs Committee of the US Congress, examining the ILO's call for an employment-generating, basic needs, income-redistribution approach to development, noted the differences between the development theories emerging during the early 1970s and conventional thinking, by pointing out that the debate was not "between advocates of growth and advocates of no growth or slow growth; it is between advocates of maximum growth in GNP regardless of how it is achieved and advocates of a growth path which puts to productive use the now underutilized labor of the poor." World Bank president Robert McNamara, in his 1973 speech to the Board of Governors in Nairobi, justified the Bank's new emphasis on reaching the poorest groups in terms of their productive potential and the contributions that the poor could make to national development.

Approaches to aid "targetting"

The international development assistance strategies that emerged during the early 1970s began to focus technical and financial assistance for the first time on an identifiable segment of the population in Third World nations. The "poor majority," or the "poorest 40 percent" of the population, or the "marginal groups" in developing societies, as they were variously referred to by international assistance organizations, were to be the "target groups" of the new assistance policies. International assistance agencies initially faced the problem of identifying and defining these beneficiaries and then of finding means of channeling aid to them. Three basic targetting strategies emerged during the 1970s: (1) aid was channeled to the places where the majority of poor lived through integrated rural development programs or rural-oriented service and production projects; (2) aid was focused on overcoming deficiencies in the living standards of the poor through basic human needs programs; and (3) aid was focused on groups with common socio-economic characteristics that created or maintained them in poverty through projects designed for "special publics."

Integrated rural development   One means of reaching the poor majority was to channel assistance to those places where the poor were concentrated. The World Bank, in its rural sector policy paper, asserted that "a special effort is needed to provide appropriate social and economic infrastructure for the rural poor and it is important to integrate these components into rural development projects. Without a concerted effort," the staff (World Bank, 1975: 5) insisted, "rural poverty will remain pervasive." The World Bank sought, by providing "minimum packages" of inputs, organizing area development programs and combining sectoral investments in rural areas, to increase agricultural productivity, expand off-farm employment and increase entrepreneurial opportunities for the rural poor.

Much like the World Bank's lending strategy, AID's program of assistance to the rural poor sought to increase productivity and income and to extend access to services and facilities to rural families who had previously been excluded from participation in productive economic activities. AID officials, responding to the "new directions" mandate from Congress, recognized in the early 1970s that traditional forms of aid for roads, irrigation, public works, and rural electrification, while necessary, were far from sufficient to increase the productivity and income of the poor. During the 1960s such investments had primarily helped larger-scale farm owners but had done little to extend the benefits to landless laborers, tenant farmers, small-farm holders and the rural unemployed, who became the primary beneficiaries of AID programs in the 1970s. AID's Working Group on the Rural Poor (USAID, 1973) contended that the more traditional projects had to be redesigned to reflect the needs of these new beneficiaries and combined with programs for human resource development, education, health, family planning, small-scale industrialization and labor-intensive agroprocessing. The access of small-holders to appropriate technology, new production inputs and markets for their products had to be increased. The Task Force on the Rural Poor insisted that USAID's strategy must include programs for creating and strengthening local institutions, such as cooperatives, farmers' organizations, municipal and district governments and regional planning units, to facilitate and coordinate service delivery. Moreover, AID strategists saw the relationships between urban and rural economies in new perspectives and called for projects that would create or strengthen linkages between rural villages, market centers, smaller cities and regional urban centers to integrate the settlement and spatial systems of developing regions. They pointed to the need for projects that would contribute to the "creation of market areas and market towns complete with services and amenities designed to make rural life productive and satisfying" (USAID, 1973: 17).

Basic human needs strategies A second approach to channeling aid to the poor emerged in the mid-1970s. United Nations Specialized Agencies, such as the International Labor Office (ILO), began calling for a new emphasis on employment generating projects that would help the world's poor overcome basic deficiencies in their standards of living and fulfill their "basic human needs." In its Declaration of Principles, the World Employment Conference, organized by the ILO in 1976, argued that previous development strategies in most developing countries had not led to a reduction of poverty and unemployment. Major shifts would be needed in both national and international development strategies to provide full employment and adequate income for the poor as quickly as possible (ILO, 1976).

The ILO defined basic needs to include two components: minimum family requirements for basic consumption such as adequate food, shelter, clothing, household equipment and furnishings; and essential community services such as potable water, sanitation, health services and educational facilities and public transport. The ILO insisted that policies for satisfying basic needs be accomplished as much as possible through self-reliant development and internal resource mobilization.

The objectives of basic needs strategies were defined in two ways. The World Bank and other assistance organizations saw the provision of basic goods and services as a precondition for increasing the productivity and income of the poor, enabling them to contribute more effectively to national development. Others such as Burki (1980: 18) argued that the aim was to "ensure the access of the poor to a bundle of essential goods and services" as a basic human right. The distinctive features of a targeting strategy for meeting basic needs in the latter sense were outlined by Streeten and Burki (1978) as follows: (a) it is concerned with meeting the needs of the poor as a legitimate goal aside from its contribution to productivity; (b) it stresses the importance of alleviating absolute poverty; (c) it emphasizes the need for supply management so that the increased income of the poor is not offset by rising prices for basic goods and services that they must purchase; (d) it emphasizes the restructuring of production so that the poor have greater access to basic goods and services despite their disadvantages in the market; (e) it is defined by characteristics of the goods and services needed by the poor rather than in terms of the goods themselves (nutritional needs rather than specific types of foods); (f) it seeks to divorce production decisions directly from market-based consumers' choices in situations where income distribution is extremely uneven; and (g) it encompasses a variety of non-material needs, such as sense of purpose in life and work, that are often satisfied as the result of obtaining material needs.

Much of China's development program during Mao's regime was aimed at providing for basic needs, creating a "floor" of income under which families would not fall, and increasing access to productive inputs through communal organization of agriculture and small industry. The success of China and some socialist countries such as Burma and Sri Lanka in this aspect of development provided evidence that basic needs approaches could be effective in alleviating or eliminating absolute poverty. They provided less impressive evidence that basic needs strategies alone could increase productivity or stimulate economic growth. (Paine, 1976; Lee, 1977; Prybyla, 1979).

Assistance to "special publics"   A third approach to channeling aid to the poor majority emerged in the mid-1970s from the realization that those living in poverty were heterogeneous groups with special characteristics, that their problems would not be alleviated entirely by general poverty policies, and that unless the productivity and income of these groups were raised, overall economic growth would be difficult to attain. World Bank officials, in their *World Development Report* for 1980, pointed out that the high levels of human development in industrialized countries were a cause as well as a result of economic growth. Developing nations, they contended, must be able to incorporate the poor with unique characteristics into productive activities through special educational, health and social services projects. "People who are unskilled or sick make little contribution to a country's economic growth," World Bank (1980: 36) analysts noted. "Development strategies that by-pass large numbers of people may not be the most effective way for developing countries to raise their long run growth rates." The report underlined the need for programs and projects that are tailored specifically to the needs of particular groups of the poor to ensure their participation. Special programs for constituent groups of the poor were necessary because, as Griffin and Khan (1978) found in their extensive studies in Southeast Asia, "poverty is associated with particular classes or groups in the community; e.g., landless agricultural laborers, village artisans, plantation workers, etc.". Yet most of the development policies and programs that had been proposed previously were "couched in terms of atomistic households in a classless society. This neo-classical assumption", they contended, "is closely associated with an assumption of universal harmony of interests."

But experience with development policies aimed at alleviating poverty continued to demonstrate that their success was often jeopardized by conflicts among groups with very different interests and that many groups living at subsistence levels had characteristics that continued to exclude them from benefits of integrated rural development and basic needs programs. Esman and Montgomery (1980: 190) called these groups "special publics" and described the circumstances that made their participation unlikely:

> These "special publics" often live in remote or hard-to-reach areas or suffer their greatest privations during the wet season, when they cannot be approached by ordinary overland routes; a few even make it a point not to be seen at public facilities set up for supplying family planning and health services, nutritional supplements, or even primary nonformal education.

Government bureaucracies that administered programs for the poor were rarely organized and equipped to deal effectively with these special publics. As Esman and Montgomery (1980: 190) noted, "for their part, the end-of-the-line field workers in a human development service are rarely motivated to break the cognitive, social and physical barriers that separate them from the special publics." The supply lines and flows of information to those working with special publics were continually interrupted. Because these groups lacked political power, their needs and demands were rarely considered in the formulation and implementation of development policies in the national capital. The only effective way of reaching these groups was to design projects that in some way were tailored to their specific needs and accounted for their special characteristics, a task with which international agencies and governments in developing countries have yet to come to grips.

CHANGING DIRECTIONS OF DEVELOPMENT POLICY

In summary, the evaluations of international assistance and development policies that were carried out during the late 1960s and early 1970s indicated that neither growth maximization and trickle down, nor semi-targetted sectoral development policies, were sufficient to overcome the growing disparities between rich and poor countries and to stimulate economic growth with social equity in developing nations. Even where conventional strategies had been successful in promoting growth in GNP they often did little to meet the needs of the majority of the poor living at or near subsistence levels who had previously been excluded from participation in economic activities. The numbers of people living in dire poverty were increasing rather than diminishing. In countries that had achieved respectable levels of economic growth with relatively equitable distribution, substantial efforts had been made prior to their period of growth to satisfy basic human needs, redistribute productive assets and intervene in market processes to assure widespread distribution and access. By 1973 international aid agencies were not only rethinking their policies and strategies, but also reformulating basic theories of development and fundamental goals of international economic assistance. The need for more precise development policies and for more effectively targetted aid strategies that would reach specific groups of the poor became more widely accepted by the early 1980s.

Ironically, just as these lessons of experience had become widely accepted, changes in international economic and political conditions raised new obstacles to applying them in developing countries. Attention shifted in the early 1980s from implementing programs to increase the income, productivity and living standards of the poor to adjusting economic structures in developing countries to allow them to cope better with severe international recession and inflation, declining demand for Third World exports, rising prices for imports and decreases in international financial assistance. The 83 percent increase in the price of oil in 1979 and 1980 alone placed extreme burdens on national budgets of petroleum-importing countries. These new costs along with substantial decreases in the flows of international assistance threatened the survival of human development projects in many countries and curtailed the ability of governments in most countries to address the problems of widespread poverty. The attention of international assistance organizations and many governments in developing nations was focused on what World Bank (1981: 8) officials called the three most important influences on their ability to survive the international economic crises: trade, energy and external finance. World Bank (1981: 14) analysts argued that the capacity of developing countries to adjust to changing economic conditions would depend on

> their ability to increase the flow of external capital and to raise the rate of domestic saving in order to finance investment aimed at restructuring their economies. Also of critical importance will be their success in increasing export growth and reducing dependence on imported oil, capital goods and raw materials.

The economic trends of the early 1980s led international economists to conclude that the "outlook for reducing poverty has worsened along with the prospects of the poor countries" (World Bank, 1981: 18). About 750 million people outside of China, for which accurate estimates were not available, were living in absolute poverty in 1980. Even under the most optimistic economic conditions – with current rates of population growth – that number could realistically be expected to decline only by 18 percent, still leaving more than 615 million people living at subsistence levels by the end of the twentieth century. Should economic growth remain sluggish, the number of desperately poor could increase to 850 million.

Despite the unanticipated and largely uncontrollable changes in the international economy that would make the development goals of the 1970s and 1980s more difficult to achieve, the lessons of experience were not entirely lost. Robert McNamara (World Bank, 1981: iii) warned that "human development is threatened during the adjustment period and the potential consequences in unnecessary human suffering are grave;" but, he argued, the "failure to deal with these problems will also have serious consequences internationally in the long term."

The changes in international economic conditions that occurred in the early 1980s were above all persistent reminders of how complex and uncertain development is. They underlined the need to find new and more effective ways of coping with unanticipated events that affect development policy-making and implementation.

NOTE

1 This chapter is a revised and expanded version of one in Kenneth Ruddle and Dennis A. Rondinelli, *Transforming Natural Resources for Human Development: A Resource Systems Framework for Development Policy*, Tokyo, United Nations University, 1983.

3

Designing development projects: the limits of comprehensive planning and management

Ironically, the planning and management procedures adopted by governments and international aid agencies for preparing and implementing development projects became more detailed and rigid at the same time that development problems were recognized as more uncertain and less amenable to systematic analysis and design.

International assistance organizations and central planning and finance ministries in developing countries adopted more detailed and complex planning procedures in an attempt to anticipate and eliminate many of the problems that plagued development activities in the past. But in attempting to apply more comprehensive and detailed controls, planners often generated new conflicts and problems. Some arose from the low levels of administrative capacity in developing nations that made it difficult for them to comply with complicated project design and selection procedures. Others evolved from disagreements over the usefulness and efficacy of those requirements. And some were the result of economic, political and social changes that could neither be anticipated nor controlled by development planners and project designers.

This chapter reviews the requirements and procedures for project planning and design that were adopted by international agencies and governments in many developing countries; explores the reasons why projects so often deviated from preconceived plans during implementation; and examines the factors that limit the usefulness of control-oriented planning and management procedures in development administration.

PROJECT PLANNING AND DESIGN PROCEDURES

International assistance agencies and most governments of developing countries have attempted to plan and control development projects through complex design, selection and appraisal procedures. The criteria to which project proposals have usually been subjected are seen in the "project cycles" that guide international agencies' activities. The

World Bank's cycle, for instance, consists of six stages through which all projects must proceed (Baum, 1978: 11):

1   *Identification:* Selection by Bank and borrowers of suitable projects that support national and sectoral development strategies and are feasible according to Bank standards. These projects are then incorporated into the lending program of the Bank for a particular country.

2   *Preparation:* The borrowing country or agency examines technical, institutional, economic and financial aspects of proposed project. Bank provides guidance, and makes financial assistance available for preparation, or helps borrower obtain assistance from other sources.

3   *Appraisal:* Bank staff review comprehensively and systematically all aspects of the project . . . and cover four major aspects: technical, institutional, economic and financial. An appraisal report is prepared on the return of Bank staff to headquarters and is reviewed extensively. This report serves as the basis for negotiations with the borrower.

4   *Negotiations:* This stage involves discussions with the borrower on the measures needed to ensure success for the project. The agreements reached are embodied in loan documents. The project is then presented to the Executive Directors of the Bank for approval. After approval the loan agreement is signed. The project can now go into its implementation stage.

5   *Implementation and Supervision:* The borrower is responsible for implementation of the project that has been agreed with the Bank. The Bank is responsible for supervising that implementation, through progress reports from the borrower and periodic field visits. An annual review of Bank supervision experience on all projects underway serves to continually improve policies and procedures. Procurement of goods and works for the project must follow official Bank guidelines for efficiency and economy.

6   *Evaluation:* An independent department of the Bank . . . reviews the completion report of the Bank's Projects Staff, and prepares its own audit of the project, often by reviewing materials at headquarters, though field trips are made where needed. This ex-post evaluation provides lessons of experience which are built into subsequent identification, preparation and appraisal work.

These cycles are relatively simple iterative planning models that have an internal logic and can be used effectively as guides to action. The problems of applying them arise from the complex requirements attached to them by international assistance organizations that are depicted in Figure 1.

Project preparation is preceded by the identification of an idea for an investment, either through formal or informal processes. In most developing countries, proposals emerge through unguided entrepreneurial investment, from programs of government ministries or agencies, or through proposals submitted by private investors for government sponsorship or participation (Rondinelli, 1976a). But regardless of their source, once an idea has been submitted, international assistance agencies have insisted that proposals be prepared in sufficient detail to test their feasibility using a complex set of financial, economic, technical and administrative criteria.

The United Nations World Health Organization (WHO), for instance, has recommended a systematic process of project analysis (Bainbridge and Sapire, 1974) prior to making a formal request for assistance. WHO's manual on project preparation requires a clear definition of the problems to be overcome by the project, identification of potential obstacles, and suggestions for changes in existing health systems to assure that project objectives are achieved and obstacles eliminated. The proposals must include an outline of all potential strategies for achieving desired results and include recommendations concerning the most feasible and effective strategy. Next, the design team is instructed to provide detailed descriptions of the selected strategy including the technology or technical procedures to be applied, the types and numbers of people to be served, staff and facility requirements such as supplies and transport, organizational structure and policy changes. Specific plans should be drawn up for obtaining funds and other resources. Once overall strategy is outlined, the design must clearly define project targets, list activities and their expected outputs, and describe the managerial and organizational arrangements and control procedures for implementation. Designers then identify and schedule project tasks, determine the implementation sequence and estimate resource requirements for each task. Finally, both life-of-the-project and annual budgets must be prepared.

The United Nations Development Program (UNDP) requires preinvestment or prefeasibility studies to determine the most appropriate means of defining an initial proposal, to gather supporting data to justify the proposal before various government agencies and review committees within UNDP, and to collect information required later for preparing a prospectus and in conducting more detailed feasibility and appraisal analyses. Generally the UNDP has suggested that preinvestment studies also identify potential bottlenecks, obstacles and preconditions for

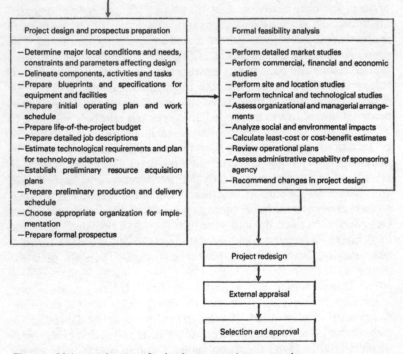

Project identification

- Perform macroanalysis: country programming, sectoral planning, forecasting and projection, policy analysis
- Perform microanalysis: gap or needs analysis, input–output studies, capital and deficiencies analysis, social analyses
- Set immediate and long-range development goals
- Set specific development targets for sectors
- Identify potential programs and projects

Initial reconnaisance and project definition

- Establish need or demand for proposed project
- Define linkages with development plans
- Determine potential "external effects" of project proposal
- Identify beneficiary groups or target areas
- Estimate "order of magnitude" costs
- Estimate other resource commitments
- Seek initial political and administrative support
- Circulate "idea stage" proposal to technical and operating ministries for review

Prefeasibility analysis and formulation

- Refine project objectives and targets
- Define potential components
- Evaluate potential design configurations
- Determine appropriate project size and potential location
- Analyze preconditions for successful implementation
- Estimate potential costs and benefits
- Prepare suggested financing plan
- Refine justification analysis
- Secure preliminary government review and approval
- Obtain preliminary review by potential funding sources

Project design and prospectus preparation

- Determine major local conditions and needs, constraints and parameters affecting design
- Delineate components, activities and tasks
- Prepare blueprints and specifications for equipment and facilities
- Prepare initial operating plan and work schedule
- Prepare life-of-the-project budget
- Prepare detailed job descriptions
- Estimate technological requirements and plan for technology adaptation
- Establish preliminary resource acquisition plans
- Prepare preliminary production and delivery schedule
- Choose appropriate organization for implementation
- Prepare formal prospectus

Formal feasibility analysis

- Perform detailed market studies
- Perform commercial, financial and economic studies
- Perform site and location studies
- Perform technical and technological studies
- Assess organizational and managerial arrangements
- Analyze social and environmental impacts
- Calculate least-cost or cost-benefit estimates
- Review operational plans
- Assess administrative capability of sponsoring agency
- Recommend changes in project design

Project redesign

External appraisal

Selection and approval

Figure 1 Major requirements for development project preparation
Source: Rondinelli (1976a).

successful execution of the project and recommend administrative and policy reforms that may be needed to implement it (Taylor, 1970; Ewing, 1974).

International assistance agencies took a greater interest in the prefeasibility stage of the project cycle in the early 1970s as a way of participating more actively in generating a greater number of what they considered to be feasible and well-prepared proposals. The World Bank, through its cooperative program, established preinvestment study agreements with the UN Food and Agriculture Organization (FAO) for agriculture and nutrition projects; the UN Educational, Scientific and Cultural Organization (UNESCO) for education and population projects; the UN Industrial Development Organization (UNIDO) on industrial projects, and with WHO on health and water supply projects and UNDP on transportation projects. The Bank in some cases prepares, and in others merely approves, the specifications and work plans for UN studies. When they are completed, the Bank reviews the preinvestment studies and then initiates its own investigations (Rondinelli, 1976a).

Depending on the form of the request and the type of project under consideration, UNDP preinvestment studies may be general investigations of sectoral or national development needs that yield potential ideas for project proposals, or they may be studies of the best way of formulating an initial idea for a project into a prospectus. If an idea has already been formulated into a preliminary proposal, the preinvestment study may involve more detailed analyses. In the prefeasibility assessment of potential agricultural projects, for example, the UNDP has required information on the volume and value of expected incremental production based on existing prices, on markets for commodities, on storage, transport, processing and distribution facilities, on price and cost incentives to producers, processors and distributors, and on the likely costs and benefits of the project. Similarly, for potential housing projects the UNDP has insisted on information about the housing market, including housing requirements within the country, effective demand and supply, distribution of income and the propensities to save of potential buyers, on available private financing and on government financing and subsidy policies (UNDP, 1973b).

USAID required from its field missions a project identification document (PID) for each proposal. It served as a preinvestment analysis by providing information on how the proposal related to USAID's assistance policies and priorities in the country, national and sectoral development objectives, a description of the beneficiaries, and the key social and economic factors that might affect the success of the project (USAID, 1974).

International assistance agencies and governments in developing countries also attempted to control the design and implementation of projects by requiring sponsors and field staff to submit detailed prospectuses as part of project formulation and preparation stages. The UNDP (1974), for instance, has used a standard "project document format" requiring a concise statement of long-range sectoral or national development criteria and immediate project objectives defined in terms of verifiable results. Project activities – the tasks that must be performed to achieve immediate objectives – are to be described in detail. Project inputs – "the resources which must be made available at specific times, in specified quantities, and in accordance with agreed specifications" – also had to be delineated. The documents had to identify the institution that would execute the project and describe its purposes, programs, financial and staff resources and organizational structure as well as its relationship to other institutions, the legal framework in which the project would operate, coordination arrangements, and provisions for government follow-up activities. Mid-project review and terminal evaluation procedures, as well as plans for subcontracting, training, procurement of equipment and supplies, provision of government contributions and operations and maintenance, all had to be specified. Each project document had to contain a detailed budget that displayed costs for all inputs as well as the expected sources of revenue. The document, depending on the size of allocations requested, was reviewed by both the UNDP Resident Representative in the developing country and headquarters staff in New York.

Similarly USAID has required for each project a set of increasingly detailed documents: initially a description of potential ideas for inclusion in Congressional budget submissions and later a project identification document that sets out the proposal in brief and identifies the resources required to design it in more detail. Finally a full-scale proposal, in the form of a Project Paper, had to be submitted. For each project submitted by field missions USAID required a project design summary or "logical framework" consisting of four sets of data: (1) the goals or objectives of the project, and the program or sector goals to which the project will contribute, in which the specific purpose of the project must be described, the intended outputs delineated and the required inputs or resources identified; (2) objectively verifiable indicators, including measures of goal achievement, conditions that will indicate at the end of the project that the purpose has been achieved, the magnitude of outputs and type and quantity of implementation targets; (3) means by which the indicators can be verified; and (4) important assumptions concerning the ability to achieve goals and targets, project purposes, and outputs, and the means of providing inputs. The logical framework required project designers to deal systematically with important management issues such as priority setting, programming, budgeting and control. The project paper also had to assess the project's technical, environmental, financial, and social soundness, and review cost and benefit implications and implementation requirements. The implementation analysis was to include: (1) a description of the recipient government's administrative arrangements for implementing the project, and an assessment of the implementing agency's potential for providing leadership, resources, commitment and "grass roots" management; (2) an implementation plan that outlines responsibilities for actions within the implementing agency and describes its relationship with other government organizations; (3) a network chart that shows the scheduling of activities over time and identifies milestones for measuring success or progress; (4) a description and discussion of potential problems or weaknesses about which reforms or policy changes should be negotiated with the government; (5) a description of proposed monitoring and evaluation techniques; (6) an analysis of logistical support required for implementation; and (7) a description of evaluation arrangements including plans for host government collaboration in evaluation, collecting baseline data, supervising progress and training evaluators.

Moreover, each international assistance agency reviewed project proposals using its own feasibility and appraisal procedures, and often required modifications in design as a result of the findings. International assistance organizations prescribed a complex set of requirements for appraising development projects. The World Bank strongly influenced the design of projects through feasibility and appraisal analyses, through formal and informal negotiations with the potential borrower before and after appraisal and through bargaining on the final loan agreement. Bank officials, attempting to exercise "leverage" on the financial and administrative procedures of developing nations, insisted that preliminary analysis and direct technical assistance were important instruments for convincing governments to modify or change design proposals. "By assisting government in the formulation of development programs and by working with borrowers to prepare high priority projects for external financing, it ensures that by the time a formal request for financing is submitted, many critical issues will already have been raised and agreements reached," the Bank's policy handbook (World Bank, 1974: 46) declared. "Through this process, up to and including the stage of project appraisal, it is often possible to introduce modifications in a project to fit sectoral priorities better, to reduce its costs, increase its efficiency or improve its financial or organizational features." The extent of the

Bank's influence on design is only hinted at by the statement that "sometimes a substitute project or one conceived on a somewhat different scale has been found to be more productive than the one originally proposed."

The World Bank used a comprehensive appraisal procedure to evaluate project proposals (Baum, 1978). Appraisal reports were usually prepared by a team of Bank economists, sometimes with assistance from outside technical experts, and included assessments of six major elements: (1) *economic aspects*, including the strength of the sector in which the project was to be undertaken, the demand for goods and services to be produced by the project, descriptions of costs and benefits, calculation of a rate-of-return, analysis of the effects of the project on balance of payments, cost analyses of potentially feasible alternatives, and least cost analyses of nonrevenue producing projects; (2) *technical aspects*, especially the engineering feasibility, appropriateness of scale and location, adequacy of manpower to prepare and supervise the project, evaluation of proposed methods and processes, layout and facility design criteria, construction scheduling and environmental consequences; (3) *managerial aspects*, including the quality of management, availability of managerial talent and experience and the need for management agents; (4) *organizational aspects*, with an assessment of the appropriateness of organizational structure for constructing and operating the project, issues of centralization versus decentralization of authority and responsibility, internal management capability in budgeting, programming and reporting, control and maintenance capacities, and adequacy of training programs; (5) *commercial aspects*, particularly the adequacy of procurement systems, availability of inputs for production, and marketing and distribution channels; and (6) *financial aspects*, including an overall evaluation of financial soundness as indicated by value of fixed assets and inventories, terms of existing debt and sources of capital, review of start-up and operating costs, and the need for and sources of new capital.

The Bank and most other assistance agencies could also insist on drastic changes through formally and informally negotiated agreements with the recipient government. These "conditions of effectiveness" for World Bank loans or "conditions precedent" in USAID project agreements required the government to make changes in the project's components, scope and organization prior to, and as a condition of, disbursement of loan or grant funds.

Negotiated agreements could be quite detailed. In a loan for a rural development project in one African country, for instance, the World Bank Group's International Development Association (IDA) insisted on conditions that specified the number and types of wells and pumps to be used in irrigation systems, the structure of the organization that would finance loans by the nation's rural development bank, and the creation of a separate management unit to execute the project. IDA also insisted on centrally consolidated accounts for the rural development fund. It set guidelines for the types of administrative and technical personnel to be hired, and prescribed mechanisms for providing extension and credit services to farmers as well as procedures for performing cost-benefit analyses in subprojects. In addition, IDA established detailed duties and responsibilities for the project manager and outlined the contents of contracts for farmers participating in the subprojects. The government was required by conditions of the loan agreement to form an interdepartmental technical committee to coordinate project activities.

Knowing that assistance organizations gave preference to projects that had high priority in government development policy and that had seemingly survived rigorous design and evaluation procedures, governments in developing nations also adopted complex formal requirements for prospectus preparation. Korea, for instance, required all proposals for government funding to follow a uniform format during the 1960s and 1970s. It described the project, estimated demand and supply for goods to be produced, provided a production schedule by year and identified intermediate inputs of domestic and foreign goods and services. In addition, the prospectus had to contain an analysis of balance of payments effects, employment schedules for construction and operating periods, costs estimates, money flowsheets by source of funds, and preliminary analyses of value-added during the project's operations (Lee, 1969).

The Nigerian government issued a manual on project preparation that outlined many design requirements. Each proposal had to contain detailed descriptions of the project's purpose, justification for its inclusion in the national investment program, the rationale for its location and details concerning assumptions and price calculations. The organizational structure had to be described in detail and sources of finance identified, including foreign and domestic funds for advance and preliminary expenditures, land, buildings, facilities, machinery, equipment, consulting services and labor. An operating budget had to be included along with macro-economic and financial analyses of the project's impact. The main technical features of the project had to be described and cost-benefit ratios calculated (Onunkwo, 1973).

The Philippine government in the mid-1970s adopted a systematic project cycle not unlike those used by international assistance agencies, to guide and control planning and implementation and to strengthen the links between national, regional and sectoral planning. It set out specific procedures for identifying, preparing, designing, appraising, managing and evaluating programs and projects (Mangahas and Subido, 1976).

THE LIMITS OF RATIONAL PLANNING AND SYSTEMATIC MANAGEMENT

A review of the experience in developing countries over the past decade confirms that — despite the complex formal requirements prescribed for project preparation, analysis, and management — projects continued to deviate widely from preconceived plans. But delays, cost overruns, changes in objectives, and other deviations are usually attributed to inadequate design, analysis, and administrative control. In a performance audit of seventy projects World Bank (1978: 3) officials found, for instance, that it was a "fairly common experience for projects to change in the course of implementation." In most cases, the officials reported, "the original design has been proven to be technically faulty or the preparation studies insufficiently detailed to foresee difficulties subsequently encountered."

But it is rarely noted that many of the problems encountered are unpredictable, no matter how comprehensively the projects were planned or how much technical analysis was done. Nor is it generally observed that detailed, rigid, and complex design, analysis, and management procedures may themselves have created many of the problems. Attempts to impose rational and systematic standards have, for instance, generated conflicts and tensions among funding agency staff, central government planners, project managers and technicians, and the various groups and organizations affected. Problems also arise from the inflexibility of planning and design procedures — especially when funding agencies attempt to force managers to follow preconceived designs in the face of unanticipated social, economic, and political changes, or when new information about existing conditions threatens the success of a project as it was originally conceived.

These problems with comprehensive planning, systematic analysis, and central control are not confined to projects in developing countries. Similar difficulties arise when governments in industrial societies attempt to plan public policies and programs in great detail (Lindblom, 1965). Attempts at comprehensive planning in the United States have often had the effect of making policies less rather than more effective (Rondinelli, 1975; Wildavsky, 1979). By focusing too heavily on objectives and procedures, planners may overestimate the resources available to carry out programs and underestimate the costs of doing detailed and systematic analysis. Comprehensive planning has often displaced dynamic processes of political interaction through which different views and perspectives could have evolved.

One needs only a cursory review of evaluations conducted by national governments and international agencies themselves in order to discover that attempts at comprehensive planning and control-oriented management generated unintended side effects that detract from the efficacy of international development projects. Attempts at systematic planning and management may result in costly but ineffective analysis; and also in greater uncertainty and inconsistency; the delegation of important development activities to foreign experts not familiar with local conditions; inappropriate interventions by central government planners; inflexibility; and unnecessary constraints on managers. Failure to include intended beneficiaries in the design and implementation of projects and reluctance to engage in the detection and correction of errors are also consequences frequently encountered.

Costly and ineffective analysis

Detailed and systematic planning is a time-consuming, costly activity that frequently entails long delays in translating policies into action and does not always ensure effective results. In reviewing the efforts of the US Agency for International Development (USAID) to design its projects in the Sahel region of Africa comprehensively, evaluators from the US General Accounting Office (USGAO, 1979: 26) noted that "the project proposals which result are not necessarily either well designed or easily implemented. The lengthy review processes produce advocacy documents which are often too theoretical to be operationally useful. The present design process is complex, requiring between 2 and 4 years for each project." The GAO's evaluation of ten projects in Senegal, Mauritania, and Niger found that more than two years were required to develop and approve project proposals; it took nearly another three months to negotiate them with the governments. In Niger USAID staff spent three years designing a livestock and range management project, only to find that outside experts and the government considered it too ambitious and that USAID's own review committee thought it too vague. The design of an integrated rural development project in Mauritania required forty months while planners attempted to collect all of the relevant data and information to design the project systematically. After a series of site visits, however, the agency's review committee decided that the proposal was not feasible and the project was revised again. Thus, after more than three years of intensive planning, it was changed to an experiment to test alternative approaches to rural development.

The project could have been initiated three years earlier and designed incrementally.

Inconsistency and increased uncertainty

Comprehensive planning and design of development projects do not necessarily reduce uncertainty, nor do they make the actions of project managers more consistent with policies and objectives. Indeed, the long delays that result from attempts at detailed planning can generate even more uncertainty and inconsistency – the very problems that systematic analysis is supposed to avoid. The rapid turnover of personnel in international funding institutions, in national ministries and agencies, and among technical consultants hired to assist with analysis and design often leads to increased inconsistency and confusion as the design process drags on. Evaluations of the . Sahel projects (USGAO, 1979: 27–8) found that "because a new team is usually recruited for each phase of the process, design consistency and efficiency are disrupted." The Senegal Casamance rural development project took two years to plan and had two entirely different design teams. The rural health improvement project in Niger required two years to plan and had three teams working on three different phases of the design. With changes of personnel conflicts developed among consultants, headquarters staff and the field personnel of the USAID Mission over concepts and components of these projects; the longer the design process dragged out, the more consensus between field personnel and headquarters staff disintegrated.

Delegation to experts and inappropriate intervention

The complexity of the procedures used to plan and analyze project proposals, together with the scarcity of highly trained technicians in most developing countries, usually results in greater dependence on foreign experts to do the required analyses and to manage the projects. But the delegation of functions to technical experts does not guarantee that the projects will be more effectively designed or more appropriate to the problems and needs of developing countries. Indeed, heavy reliance on foreign consultants, who presumably understand and can meet the requirements of the international agency, often leads to projects that are unrealistic and inappropriate for local conditions. Such delegation during the 1960s and 1970s, for instance, led to projects based on incorrect assumptions concerning local capabilities and constraints which later contributed to serious problems of implementation (Noranitipadungkarn,

1977). In other cases inappropriate methods have been applied by technical experts who were not familiar with the culture of the country in which they were working and who designed projects that were not suited to its needs.

Moreover, these complex methods of feasibility analysis, appraisal, and selection may introduce a bias toward the choice of projects that are easy to analyze, but are of low priority for development. The insistence of international agencies on using complex feasibility analyses, for example, often leads consultants and governments to propose large-scale, high-technology, capital construction projects because they are considered to be more worthy than smaller, labor-intensive, social and human resource development programs of the time, effort, manpower, and funds that must be invested in elaborate and detailed analysis. Frequently the delegation of project planning and design to international consultants results in projects that meet approved technical and financial analysis requirements, but that are either ineffective in solving local problems or produce adverse consequences (Strachan, 1978; Thomas, 1974).

Failure to involve intended beneficiaries in planning and management

Many of the planning and management procedures adopted by international agencies and governments of developing countries during the 1960s and 1970s originated with multinational corporations and engineering firms that had developed them to analyze and manage capital construction and weapons systems projects. They conferred an aura of scientific precision that encouraged administrators to search for quantitative solutions to problems and to rely on technical standards rather than to seek knowledge and insights from those who were supposed to benefit from the social or economic development programs. Few of the two hundred rural development projects funded by the United Nations Development Program (UNDP) during the 1970s, for instance, elicited the participation of the people for whom they were intended. In many rural areas, the long-standing and deeply ingrained distrust between rural people and government officials prevented either side from taking the other into its confidence. The systems management approach adopted by the governments of some developing countries reinforced the paternalistic attitudes of central government officials toward the rural poor and in the minds of the administrators obviated the need to include beneficiaries in project planning and implementation. Only in about one-third of all the UNDP's rural development projects were local involvement or resource contributions equal to those called for in the original proposals. Less than one-quarter of the projects had any effective participation by local residents, and almost none involved the beneficiaries in evaluation. The failure to include beneficiaries in the design and formulation of projects often led to severe management problems later. For instance, projects were assigned to the wrong organizations for implementation, or to one with insufficient administrative and technical capacity to carry it out, or to one so tightly controlled by vested interest groups that it could not serve the intended beneficiaries (UNDP, 1979).

The transfer of inappropriate technology is another indication of the lack of knowledge or sufficient concern about local conditions and needs. Evaluators of UNDP-sponsored rural development projects found that "a major constraint affecting achievement of project objectives is the transfer of technologies without local adaptation." The complex technology that administrators often recommend may have little or no advantage over less complex indigenous methods or equipment. Evaluators have argued that "even if there is an advantage, it is often nullified by lack of understanding or by resentment of a new idea 'parachuted' into an area without previous consultation with the users."

Inflexibility and unnecessary constraints on managers

There is not much evidence to support the contention that highly detailed, preconceived designs and centrally controlled management systems make projects easier to implement. Indeed, the difficulty of managing development projects according to detailed preconceived designs was pointed up in the GAO's review of the Sahel projects: "The magnitude of the AID project managers' tasks is enormous. They are to manage the transfer of technical assistance – new knowledge and technology – to the Sahel people. Yet many of the Sahel people are poorly educated and are oriented to tribal customs not all AID development programmers fully understand" (USGAO, 1979: 5). The conditions under which the projects must be implemented are often so constraining that field managers cannot adhere to the preconceived designs; nor can they quickly change these conditions to make them compatible with the plans. The people to whom they must deliver new knowledge and technology, as the USGAO (1979: 5) analysts discovered,

> live in harsh environments endemic to [sic] crippling and even killing diseases, having little or no means of outside communication. Achieving significant program objectives quickly is extremely difficult when these environmental problems are coupled with such other project

implementation difficulties as the Sahel governments' inability to adequately support project goals, slow arrival of equipment, supplies and technical expertise and ineffective use of the AID project evaluation system.

Under these conditions, the most valuable managerial skill is not necessarily the ability to conform to preconceived project plans or project schedules, but the ability to innovate, experiment, modify, improvise, and lead – talents that are often discouraged or suppressed by rigid designs and centrally controlled management procedures. What leads to success is the ability of managers to design and manage simultaneously, and to test new ideas and methods continuously no matter what the circumstances in which they find themselves. This managerial flexibility, however, is often squashed by officials in headquarters of international agencies or national ministries who insist on conformance to detailed plans and rigid management systems. In such situations the major criterion of success for many project managers turns on their ability to conform to plans or programs designed in aid agency or national ministry headquarters, rather than on their ability to seize local opportunities in order to achieve a project's purposes or to modify goals to reflect changing or unanticipated conditions.

Reluctance to engage in evaluation and error detection

Finally, administrators in developing countries and international assistance agencies have a limited capacity to discover when and how projects stray from their designed paths during implementation. The emphasis on meeting schedules and achieving detailed objectives makes them reluctant to uncover and correct mistakes. Often, sponsoring agencies or funding institutions fail to plan for monitoring and evaluation; thus, they do not know when they deviate from the plans or what the ultimate effects are on beneficiaries. Few undertakings sponsored by international assistance agencies include provisions for collecting simple baseline data prior to the start of the project and for collecting information to measure progress during its execution (APHA, 1977). The UNDP (1979: 27) found that in most of its two hundred projects "baseline data were usually missing, and in those agricultural projects where outputs were clearly specified, most were related to increased aggregate production without assessing distributional effects." As a result, the success of many projects was measured by resources expended or inputs used during implementation, rather than by the quality and quantity of outputs, the impact of results on beneficiaries, or the nature of changes attributable to a project's successful operation.

Although the UNDP, World Bank, AID and other international organizations as well as many governments of developing countries have elaborate project evaluation procedures and prescribe monitoring and review of ongoing projects, evaluation is less rigorous and accurate than headquarters procedures imply because of this absence of baseline data and the inherent difficulties of measuring actual results and impacts on intended beneficiaries. Kilby (1979: 309) points out that it is usually "in the interests of all parties to conclude that, save for the most visible failures, every project attains an acceptable level of success." The desire of administrators to place their projects in the most favorable light, and the unwillingness of international organizations to embarrass recipient governments, also inhibits accurate evaluation. Thus, the reluctance of administrators to engage in error detection and correction makes it difficult for anyone to know when projects are deviating from their planned paths; it reduces the ability of managers to learn from past mistakes and limits their capacity to redesign projects when they meet obstacles or difficulties.

CONSTRAINTS ON MAKING SYSTEMATIC ANALYSIS, COMPRE-HENSIVE PLANNING AND CONTROL-ORIENTED ADMINISTRATION MORE EFFECTIVE

Some development administrators have argued that the systematic methods of planning, analysis, and management adopted by international agencies and many national governments did not work because they were not seriously tried. But in view of the dynamic environment of political and social interaction that affects development activities and the complex and uncertain nature of development problems, deviation from plans must be expected. Moreover, conditions in developing nations make it highly unlikely that systematic and centrally controlled management procedures can be made more effective.

In fact, the uncertainty of development problems and the complexity of relationships between developing nations and international assistance organizations make it nearly impossible to plan, analyze and manage projects in highly rational and systematic ways. The attempt to impose such procedures often creates adverse results. The most serious constraints include: difficulties in defining project objectives precisely at the outset; lack of appropriate data and information; inadequate understanding of local social and cultural conditions; weak incentives or controls for guiding the behavior of participants in project implementation; the dynamics of political interaction and intervention; and the developing countries' low levels of administrative capacity to plan and manage in the prescribed ways.

Difficulties of defining objectives and goals precisely

One of the most frequently cited obstacles to the more effective management of development projects is the imprecision of their goals and objectives. Evaluators for the UNDP (1973), for instance, reported that in many of the technical assistance projects undertaken in Nigeria, objectives were stated so vaguely or imprecisely that funding agency staff, government officials, project managers, consultants and participants were in continual conflict over the most efficient ways of managing them. Another UNDP (1974: 27) study found general confusion "regarding the meaning of long-term and immediate objectives, outputs, and workplans. . . . Similarly, immediate objectives (project effects) were commonly confused with measurable outputs, and sometimes with elements of the workplan which was often in the nature of a reporting schedule." The American Public Health Association (APHA, 1977: 11) reviewing 180 health projects in developing countries for USAID, found that "large proportions of the projects appear to be engaged in [the pursuit of] a variety of objectives that are largely implicit and unarticulated."

In most cases it is difficult or impossible to define goals and objectives precisely at the outset, or to give more than general indications of what can be accomplished when a proposal is initially made – especially for social and human resource development projects in rural areas. USAID (1975: 5) officials have admitted the difficulty of "tracing out exactly who is affected by an activity and what the long-range consequences are." USAID Missions expressed their frustration over their inability to quantify the needs of the poorest groups in developing countries. As the staff of the Philippine Mission pointed out, "poverty is an elusive concept. Many definitions and measures have been advanced. All have limitations in methodology and applicability to specific countries' established social values." It is nearly impossible to specify goals for projects aimed at increasing the living standards of the poor when "essential factors of poverty, like dietary habits, housing standards, price differentials and ecological diversity are yet to be explored in any great detail." Specific goals often cannot be identified until activities are well under way and the conditions under which they will be implemented are better known. The best that can be done at the outset of a project is to state objectives generally and to aim at broad targets.

The insistence of funding organizations – whether they be international aid agencies or central government ministries – on precise and detailed statements of objectives at the outset in order to facilitate systematic planning, management and control often leads to game-playing, phony precision and inaccurate reporting that create severe administrative problems later on. In his evaluation of eleven United Nations technical assistance projects for developing small-scale industry and handicraft cooperatives, Kilby (1979: 316–17) found that many of the initial proposals did indeed lack specific goals and targets. But he also noted that the planners and administrators who designed the proposals often unrealistically enlarged the goals and targets that they could identify. Unable to predict precisely what the projects could achieve, but faced with demands for quantitative indicators, administrators overestimated the number of people who would find jobs through project activities by more than five times the actual number who were eventually employed.

Administrators faced either with conforming to requirements for systematic planning and precise identification of objectives and goals (regardless of their capacity to do so) or with losing funding for a project, often provide seemingly precise statements that are inaccurate, unverifiable or mere window dressing. The objectives are often the ones that planners *think* the funding organizations want rather than those that administrators can achieve. Moreover, projects are often designed by central government officials, international agency staff or foreign consultants who will not ultimately be responsible for managing them, and who may be more concerned with formulating a "fundable" proposal than with planning a project that is administratively feasible (Ahmad, 1977).

Lack of appropriate or adequate data

Systematic planning and management procedures often require information and data that are simply not available in most developing countries. Such demands may force administrators to use whatever data are at hand, regardless of their appropriateness or accuracy. Requirements that USAID projects be targetted on the poorest groups in developing countries led some missions to complain during the 1970s that the precise information needed to get projects approved and to ensure desired results simply did not exist or was not easy to acquire. The USAID (1979: 7) Mission in Pakistan, for example, reported that "the identification of depressed economic groups is beset by problems of serious data scarcity." The USAID (1979a: i) staff in Sri Lanka noted that the "socio-economic data base – while at first glance ample – contains serious deficiencies." The USAID (1979b: 2) Mission in

Burma pointed out that "to a Burmese, *sinye* (to be poor) implies the absence of resources but it also describes a distressed mental state related to material status. . . . The Burmese have never defined poverty in economic terms. With the paucity of data, the international donors have also been loath to undertake this arduous task."

But collecting more data and information will not by itself overcome problems of project management. Nor will it necessarily make implementation more rational and systematic. Indeed, Chambers and Belshaw (1973) observe in their study of the Special Rural Development Program in Kenya that the tendency to collect all conceivably useful data created confusion about purposes, and inhibited managers from learning while they implemented the projects.

Inadequate understanding of social and cultural conditions

Another serious limitation on systematic, control-oriented planning and management is the difficulty of comprehending at the outset of a project all of the social and cultural nuances that are important for effective administration. The demand for systematic analysis and management often leads planners and administrators to use information and data that can be easily gathered or manipulated by statistical methods. This misplaced priority on quantification often makes the planning and analytical procedures of international assistance agencies or national ministries ends in themselves. In the detailed feasibility studies required by the World Bank, analysts often manipulate vast amounts of unreliable data with complex statistical formulas in order to reach a conclusion on the desirability or undesirability of a project. It is likely that officials of the host governments could have assessed the project at a fraction of the time and expense by drawing on their experience and knowledge of local conditions.

The more sophisticated the analytical requirements, the more likely essential nonquantifiable information will be overlooked. Many agricultural development projects sponsored by USAID during the 1960s and 1970s were identified from linear programming models, but many of the resulting proposals for assistance projects to small farmers failed to include information that was vital to the success of the project. It had simply never been collected and quantified. The analyses of projects in Guatemala, for example, did not account for cost or profit conditions of the farmers for whom the projects were intended; farmers had this information, but it was never solicited from them. The project designers simply assumed that increased agricultural productivity would generate larger profits, an assumption that turned out to be highly questionable.

The projects thus did little to improve production or raise the incomes of Guatemalan peasants (Hutchinson *et al.*, 1974).

The tendency to design projects without adequate knowledge of local conditions and needs is not confined to those involving foreign consultants. Administrators in central government ministries often know as little as some external consultants about minority ethnic, regional or religious groups within their own countries. Or they may fail to incorporate what is known into project designs because the information cannot be quantified. An evaluation of eight settlement and livestock projects in the Sudan, for instance, concluded that all of them had had problems obtaining the acceptance and cooperation of local residents. Those that had been designed to settle nomadic groups ran into special difficulties. "Social acceptance became a particular problem in irrigation projects where nomads were expected to be available for scheduled work in their fields at time periods which apparently clashed with their livestock herding interests," Thimm (1979: 48) reports. The nomads simply opposed the managers of the projects, even though the pasture conditions in the area were technically suitable to make the program a success. In nearly all cases, the projects had been designed by central government planners who knew little about local conditions and who made few attempts to discover or understand the cultural practices that would be essential to successful implementation.

Weak incentives or controls to guide behavior

In many cases, international agencies and central government ministries lack the incentives or controls to change or redirect the behavior of participants. Too much is simply beyond them.

Credit projects for small farmers sponsored by USAID in Latin America during the 1970s, for example, were not very successful because managers could not change the lending practices of local financial institutions, which simply refused to lend to small farmers. Lenders considered the farmers poor credit risks and feared that if they changed their policies they would alienate their large-scale farmer clientele who wielded considerable political influence and were not interested in promoting greater competition or improving the lot of the small farmers. In her evaluation of such projects in Ecuador and Honduras, Tendler (1976: 31–3) notes that there was very little relationship between changes in institutional practices and renewals of USAID assistance, even though "the design of current AID loan programs results in a very low probability that promised changes in the institution's behavior will actually occur, once the loan agreement has been signed." She concludes:

> If AID wants to lend to institutions that are not behaving in the desired way, and expects to bring about changes in those behaviors, it must impose costs on the behaviors it wishes to change. It must make them dysfunctional, instead of functional, to the recipient institutions.

Even the World Bank, which explicitly uses its lending "leverage" to force changes in economic and institutional practices in developing countries as a condition for approving projects, admits that significant institutional changes are often the most difficult to achieve. Institutional reforms have been included in many projects designed by the Bank, but the staff recognizes that "whereas the physical objectives have generally been achieved, and this can clearly be determined, the institutional objectives are both less frequently attained and their attainment less easily measured" (World Bank, 1978: 8).

Dynamics of political interaction and intervention

Among the most severe constraints on planning and managing development projects in rational and systematic ways is the inevitable political intervention and conflict that will arise in the process. Serious differences of opinion among government officials, funding agency staff, consultants and participants are often deliberately repressed or ignored when a project is proposed, so that it will be reviewed and approved expeditiously. These differences later erupt as conflicts that can affect the course of implementation. Or there may be a turnover of key personnel within the executing agency or funding institution after a proposal is formulated, submitted and approved that brings in new staff who do not understand, or who disagree with, the original design. They may attempt to alter, modify or circumvent the provisions of the agreement.

Sometimes after proposals have been submitted and approved by funding agencies and recipient governments, one side or the other becomes disillusioned when the details or management implications emerge. An audit of a USAID-sponsored insect-control agricultural project in Tunisia noted that "there has never been a full meeting of the minds by all interested parties on the purposes of the project and the responsibilities of the respective governments." In the early stages all were agreed on the desirability of ridding Tunisia of fruit flies, but the US Department of Agriculture's technicians were primarily interested in testing techniques potentially applicable in the United States and the

Western hemisphere. After the details became known, the Tunisian government was so unimpressed with the economic benefits to be derived in its ccuntry that it would agree to further participation only if the United States bore the full cost. Another project was cancelled by the Moroccan government because of similar differences in perception about its purposes and methods (USAID: 1973a).

Conflicts can also arise from the politics of project formulation and negotiation. Although international assistance agencies insist that projects be appraised and selected on the basis of objective financial and technical criteria, political leaders often intervene to shape a project's scope, components and organizational arrangements. That is especially true in the case of large, high-priority development projects, or those in which a government thinks that its sovereignty is being impinged upon by international agencies. Thus – despite the elaborate search, identification and selection procedures employed by most international assistance agencies – one evaluation of United Nations assistance projects in Africa and Asia pointed out that "in practice project selection tends to be heavily influenced by considerations which are extraneous to a rational screening process." The two major factors that often sway decisions are "the immediate socio-political events which lead up to the project request and the personal background of the UN advisers assisting in project identification and project formulation" (Kilby, 1979: 312).

In his study of UN-sponsored projects in Malawi, Tanzania and Zambia, Gordenker (1976) notes that presidents and prime ministers in each country intervened directly in negotiations on large projects; sometimes they deliberately generated conflicts with international agency personnel in order to obtain concessions or greater control over design and implementation. The design and funding of the Botswana Nickel-Copper Mines project, for example, involved a long, tortuous process of political bargaining; for more than a decade, the Prime Minister played an important role in negotiating with the World Bank and a group of private investors to reach a mutual compromise (Ostrander, 1974). The final proposal was less a reflection of formal principles of "good management" than a bundle of political compromises minimally acceptable to all parties.

Low levels of administrative capacity

Finally, attempts at systematic analysis and comprehensive planning often lead planners to "overdesign" projects; that is, they are made too complex or sophisticated for the institutions assigned to implement them. Methods of analysis used by national planners or the staffs of international agencies are often imposed on indigenous organizations. In the small-farmer credit and cooperative projects in Ecuador and Honduras funded by USAID, designers required farmers' organizations to use complicated auditing and bookkeeping methods, which they could not perform adequately; nor were they willing to pay for such services. Their ability to take advantage of programs sponsored by the cooperative federation was therefore severely limited (Tendler, 1976).

Governments in the Sahel region of Africa have never been able to absorb and support the extensive technical and financial assistance provided by aid agencies to that poverty-stricken region. The Sahel governments had neither the administrative capacity nor the matching funds needed to make the projects designed by USAID work effectively. Their inability to provide contributions at agreed-upon levels left the projects and the overall development plan for the Sahel in disarray during the 1970s. The Sahel governments were not able to recruit managers for many of the projects until two or three years after they had been approved; inordinate delays occurred in providing routine administrative authority to project directors once they had been appointed. Foreign technicians therefore often had no national counterparts until late in their assignments and were thus not able to train them before their departure (USGAO, 1979).

The ability of technical experts and project managers to follow a detailed project design once they are on the job may also be extremely limited. In his evaluation of eleven technical assistance projects sponsored by United Nations agencies, (Kilby, 1979: 313) points out that "effective operation of these experts was hampered by under-provision of counterparts, language problems, lack of logistical support from the Ministry and shifting government policy." In some cases, the government altered its requests or demanded changes in the scope or content of a project after it had gotten underway because scarce technical and managerial personnel had to be reassigned to other projects or activities. Moreover, long delays in receiving essential equipment or supplies often slowed down the projects or changed their fundamental nature, requiring unanticipated alterations in activities and outputs.

Projects designed and prepared by headquarters staff of international agencies and by central ministries in developing countries often require high levels of coordination among government agencies and between the public and private sectors in the developing states. Yet the ability of central planning agencies and government ministries to coordinate and control their resources is extremely weak in most cases. The evaluation of UNDP (1979: 21) rural development projects pointed out that "coordination between government departments in concepts and actions is enormously complicated by sectoral factionalism" – a problem aggravated by the sectoral specializations within the United Nations system. "The compartmentalization between technical line ministries and their relationships to the ministries of planning and finance finds a virtual mirror image in the UN system of Specialized Agencies and their relationship to the UNDP Resident Representative in the field."

TOWARD A REORIENTATION OF DEVELOPMENT ADMINISTRATION

All of these problems raise serious questions about the value of attempts to plan and analyze proposals comprehensively and systematically and to design projects in great detail prior to their implementation. The argument being made, however, is *not* that planning and analysis should not be done – or done with great care and in detail – but that existing methods, procedures and requirements that place strong priority on comprehensive planning and design during the preparatory stages of the project cycle are misplaced, inappropriate and often perverse. The complexity of development problems, the variety of factors that must be taken into account and dealt with during implementation, and the inherent uncertainty about the outcome of all development projects suggest that alternative methods of planning and implementation must be employed.

The remaining chapters, therefore, begin to explore an adaptive approach, based on concepts of strategic planning, incremental analysis, experimental design and successive approximation in decision-making.

4

Implementing development projects as policy experiments: toward adaptive administration

If control-oriented planning and management are neither effective nor appropriate in coping with complexity and uncertainty, what alternatives do planners and administrators have for dealing with development problems more effectively? One way of coping with uncertainty, complexity and ignorance is to recognize that all development projects are policy experiments and to plan them incrementally and adaptively by disaggregating problems and formulating responses through a process of decision-making that joins learning with action. Adaptive administration allows planners to perform what Wildavsky (1979: 15) calls the basic task of policy analysis: "to create problems that decision-makers are able to handle with the variables under their control and in the time available." Planning and implementation are thus an art, "an activity creating problems that can be solved" through informed trial and error. Courses of action are shaped from lessons of past experience as well as from a more realistic understanding of current and emerging conditions.

This chapter describes a four-stage process of project planning and implementation that seeks to cope with problems in an experimental, incremental and adaptive fashion. The framework depicted in Figure 2 directs the attention of planners and administrators to issues about which little is known or about which there is usually a great deal of uncertainty. By planning and implementing projects sequentially through experimental, pilot, demonstration and replication phases, problems can be effectively disaggregated and alternative courses of action can evolve through what Korten (1981: 214–16) considers to be the three basic stages of learning: (1) learning to be *effective* in assisting intended beneficiaries to improve their living conditions or to attain other development goals; (2) learning to be *efficient* in eliminating ineffective, unnecessary, overly costly or adverse activities, and identifying methods that are appropriate for larger-scale application; and (3) learning to *expand* the application of effective methods by creating appropriate and responsive organizations to carry out development tasks.

	Project type or stage			
	Experimental	Pilot	Demonstration	Replication or production
Unknowns or design problems	Problem or objective			
	Possible alternative solutions			
	Methods of analysis or implementation	Methods of analysis or implementation		
	Appropriate technology	Appropriate technology		
	Required inputs or resources			
	Adaptability to local conditions	Adaptability		
	Transferability or replicability	Transferability		
			Replicability	
	Acceptability by local populations	Acceptability	Acceptability	
	Dissemination or delivery systems	Dissemination or delivery systems	Dissemination or delivery systems	Dissemination or delivery systems
				Large-scale production technology

Characteristics Higher ———————————————————————————— Lower

- — — — Uncertainty and risk — — — — — — — — — — — — — — —
- — — — Political vulnerability — — — — — — — — — — — — — —
- — — — Innovativeness — — — — — — — — — — — — — —
- — — — Addition to existing knowledge — — — — — — — — — —
- — — — Need for creative management — — — — — — — — — —
- — — — Need for flexibility of organizational structure — — — — — —
- — — — Need for rare or specialized technical skills — — — — — —

Figure 2 A framework for adaptive administration of development projects
Source: Rondinelli (1979b).

This chapter describes the characteristics of each phase in the adaptive administration of development projects. Illustrations are drawn from actual projects, even though many of those cited were not planned and managed entirely by an adaptive process and did not always complete the four phases from experimentation to replication. The use of a sequential, four-phased process of decision-making does not imply that decisions should be always conceived of as linear, or that projects must always evolve through all four phases. Enough is often known about objectives, probable effects, the conditions under which they will be carried out, and the characteristics of their beneficiaries so that some projects can skip or place less emphasis on some stages. Nor does it assume that development planners and administrators begin every project "empty headed and empty handed." It seeks to provide a framework by which planners and administrators can make use of what they already know and to test the appropriateness of that knowledge in coping with new problems, under different conditions. The framework is only useful – as is any planning process, management technique or method of analysis – as an aid to judgment. It can assist decision-makers in coping with problems in a more manageable form, to take actions that are grounded in experience and to adapt them to conditions and needs of particular groups of people in specific places to arrive at more responsive decisions – the effectiveness of which, inevitably, remains uncertain.

EXPERIMENTAL PROJECTS

Experimental projects are generally small-scale, highly exploratory, risky ventures that do not always provide immediate or direct economic returns or yield quick and visible results. Their benefits are derived from the acquisition of knowledge. They can be useful in defining (or "creating," as Wildavsky would say) development problems, finding more useful ways of coping with basic social needs, assessing a broad range of possible interventions, and exploring the conditions under which development projects must operate. Thus, experimental projects are needed when problems are not well-articulated, elements or characteristics of a problem have not been clearly identified, alternative courses of action have not been widely explored and their impacts cannot be easily anticipated. Under these conditions, effective management methods and techniques cannot be confidently prescribed. Little is known about the appropriate types, amounts and combinations of resources or about the most effective sequence and timing of interventions.

By formulating development projects through a phased, experimental approach, as was South Korea's village development program, *Saemaul Undong*, information can be gathered from a few places, or from a large number of places about a few activities, before embarking on a demonstration or full-fledged national program. During the experimental phases of *Saemaul Undong*, the national government offered all villages a limited amount of building materials with which to launch small self-help projects. The experience of both successful and less successful communities was analyzed to determine how they organized self-help activities, how they identified and selected leaders, what forms of cooperation they used, and what kinds of government support would be needed to promote self-help projects requiring more extensive cooperation among villagers (Kim and Kim, 1977; Kim, 1978).

Experimental projects can be used to assess, simultaneously or sequentially, alternative courses of action and to allocate resources to those that seem most feasible during early phases of testing or observation. Experimental projects can be used to test the applicability of methods and techniques that are transferred from other countries or sectors. If problems arise from unique cultural or ecological conditions, as is often the case in agricultural, population and manpower development projects, experiments can search for courses of action that are especially well suited to local constraints.

Moreover, experimental projects can lower the risk of innovating. Cuca and Pierce (1977) conclude from their analyses of family planning programs that the costs and threats of failure can be kept small. Different techniques, combinations of inputs and organizational arrangements can be tested on a limited scale or in only a few places. If the experiments do not succeed, other approaches can be tried quickly without wasting large amounts of money or unduly embarrassing the government and the sponsoring organization. Small experimental failures may not threaten the survival of a larger program. In addition, experimentation sets in motion a learning process. "The experiments generated new questions that became the subject of subsequent experiments," Cuca and Pierce (1977: 4) found, and "family planning experiments have also contributed to the development of their own methodology."

But experience indicates that complex social projects cannot be designed as classical scientific or behavioral experiments in which populations are divided into test and control groups, baseline measures are taken, "treatments" are administered, and the differences due to "treatment" are determined. Chambers and Belshaw (1973) observed in the Special Rural Development Program (SRDP) in Kenya that it was difficult, if not impossible, to establish valid experimental and control groups in each area. Different ecological, social, economic and physical conditions made comparison difficult even in relatively homogeneous regions. Moreover, the "before and after" effects of projects may take years to observe, and changes can be attributed to causes other than the experiments. Problems of finding comparable control areas were also reported in the Comilla Project in Bangladesh (Choldin, 1969), where the ability to conduct classical scientific experiments was further limited by political pressures and administrative constraints. Project staff were required to modify their activities quickly when unanticipated problems arose or when technical problems made preconceived courses of action impossible to follow. Of course, it was not possible to control the behavior of participants sufficiently to determine the experiments' precise impact.

Because of the constraints on using a scientific approach, the term "experiment" must be defined more loosely. A broad definition was used in the SRDP in Kenya: trying alternative strategies for attaining specific objectives by organizing projects to show if the strategies work and, if so, how well (IDS, 1972). SRDP, which compared rural development techniques in different areas, was based on three principles: that it was possible to distinguish among strategies and to attribute results to them; that strategies must have clearly defined objectives, implying the need for criteria by which to assess successes and failures; and, that objectives should be defined in measurable terms so that the extent of their success could be determined.

Defined broadly, there are at least five types of experimental projects:

1   Those that focus on *problem definition* either make no presupposition about the nature of a problem or assume that all previous descriptions of problems or courses of action are erroneous or inappropriate. Usually the experiments examine the "symptoms" that indicate dissatisfaction or the existence of a problem. The project is used to diagnose characteristics or aspects of a problem from which possible courses of action can be identified. For instance, the Puebla project, which began the "Green Revolution" in Mexico, started with the assumption that little was known about agricultural conditions in sub-tropical and high altitude areas and that existing cultivation techniques and extension programs were not appropriate. Experimental projects were needed to define problems more accurately and to tailor programs to the subsistence agricultural conditions found in such climates.

2   Some experimental projects focus on "*unknowns*." They seek solutions to problems that are only partially defined. The knowledge gained through experimental activities is used to refine definitions or to distinguish among elements of the problem in different areas.

The experience of the Pakistan Academy for Rural Development with the Daudzai project – which sought to provide basic social and health services, upgrade human skills and integrate service delivery in rural areas of Peshawar – confirmed the value of experimental and pilot projects for these purposes. Officials noted that the "Academy learned very important lessons from this experience," the most important of them being that "rural people were in the best position to identify their own needs because they had been living in the villages for generations and no one else could be sensitive and alive to their needs" (Khan, 1978: 142). Planners found that rural people were often better able to suggest solutions to local problems than were *markaz officials*. The plans that emerged from experimental and participatory activities were far different than those designed previously without popular participation by local officials. Surveys and reconnaissance studies made planners realize that the needs of villages differed substantially from each other and that unless the process was experimental, probing, and participatory it would be impossible to plan appropriate or responsive projects for village development (Khan, 1978).

3   Other experiments seek the most effective means of attaining *objectives* that are already well defined. Goals may be stated broadly and the problem is to determine the most appropriate means of achieving them. Planners of the SRDP projects in Kenya, for example, had determined that rural poverty in that country was due to low levels of income, poor standards of living and the lack of self-sustaining economic activities. Thus, the immediate objective of SRDP was to fill productivity and equity gaps. The projects explored alternative ways of increasing marketable agricultural output, increasing wage employment, improving public services and decentralizing the planning and administration of government programs. Some experiments sought to increase output through agricultural, commercial or industrial enterprises, reduce unemployment through public works projects or by creating private enterprises, improve public services through extension, training, social, health and educational programs, and increase popular participation in decision-making at the district and local government levels. Those alternatives found useful in the experimental phases became prototypes for pilot and demonstration projects.

4   In situations where both problems and objectives are clearly perceived, experimental projects may be used to discover and break bottlenecks or to overcome *deficiencies*. Again, the SRDP projects in Kenya serve as an example. Earlier research discovered the

constraints inhibiting rural development, and planners concluded that it was the lack of knowledge, skills and resources available for increasing agricultural production and employment opportunities in nonagricultural sectors, inadequate marketing facilities and physical and organizational infrastructure in rural areas, ineffective planning and control procedures in local administration, and inadequate funding for local programs and projects that kept rural people in poverty. Many of the SRDP projects, therefore, were designed to test methods of overcoming these deficiencies: extension programs, informal training and formal educational schemes were proposed; new organizational arrangements were introduced in rural areas to elicit popular participation and to mobilize resources. New planning and management procedures were tested. Planners experimented with appointing district and area development supervisors, designating "linkmen" in relevant ministries to expedite action on project proposals and to implement programs, introducing new methods of staff deployment, creating local development committees and setting aside extra funds for local experiments. New equipment was provided to local administrators and they were given opportunities for special training.

Saemaul Undong, Korea's program for raising living standards in rural communities, used a village classification scheme to identify and overcome deficiencies inhibiting development. Planners found that in "underdeveloped villages," basic infrastructure was missing, organizational arrangements for cooperation were weak or nonexistent, housing conditions were poor and local leaders were not active in community affairs. The government encouraged basic infrastructure and farm-to-market road projects in these villages and provided housing improvement assistance and aid in establishing cooperatives (Republic of Korea, 1980). All of these projects had to be implemented by the villagers themselves in order to build community spirit and promote local leadership. The government provided guidance, materials and standards. In "developing villages," where basic infrastructure, housing and income were adequate, *Saemaul Undong* provided assistance in increasing agricultural production. Building bridges and meeting halls, upgrading farm roads, constructing small-scale irrigation facilities and establishing credit unions, would all require stronger cooperation among villagers. The projects had to be organized by local Saemaul leaders who could obtain technical assistance and materials from the government. Finally, in "developed villages," where infrastructure, housing conditions and services were above average,

Saemaul Undong concentrated on promoting income-generating and community welfare projects. The development of group farming, off-season vegetable cultivation, common market facilities and rural factories was encouraged.

These experiments tested different combinations of activities and allowed villages to proceed from simple to more complex projects only after fundamental deficiencies were overcome and arrangements for cooperation and local resource mobilization were established. This approach allowed Saemaul leaders to identify and solve different types of problems in villages at different levels of development. It started with small projects that focused on overcoming basic deficiencies and that built community spirit and channels of cooperation and went on to expand capacity to take on more diversified and larger scale projects.

5   Finally, since most development programs cannot be designed and carried out as controlled experiments, learning must be derived from "*natural experiments.*" As Choldin (1969) notes in his description of the Comilla Project in Bangladesh, "the natural experiment involves the historical analysis of a situation to understand the dynamics of previous events," and to incorporate the lessons of successful experiments into other projects with similar objectives. Most often, such projects were not designed to be experiments, but turned out to be tests of important methods, approaches or principles of development. Some were spontaneous, but yielded lessons for deliberate efforts to achieve the same results.

Korten's (1980) studies of the Indian National Dairy Development Board, the Sarvodaya Shramadana Movement in Sri Lanka, Bangladesh's Rural Advancement Committees, the Community-Based Family Planning Services in Thailand, and the National Irrigation Administration's Communal Irrigation Program in the Philippines were analyses of natural experiments. They not only offered lessons about how to organize projects to be responsive to local needs but provided insights into the characteristics of natural experiments. Korten (1980: 497) contends that:

these five programs were not designed and implemented – rather they emerged out of a learning process in which villagers and program personnel shared their knowledge and resources to create a program which achieved a fit between needs and capacities of the beneficiaries and those of outsiders who were providing assistance. Leadership and team work, rather than blueprints, were the key elements. Often the individuals who emerged as central figures were involved at the very initial stage in this village experience, learning at first hand the nature of the beneficiary needs and what was required to address them effectively.

Administrators were responsive to changes in local conditions, needs and capacities and thus the assistance programs emerged from "a learning process in which research and action were integrally linked."

The lessons of these natural experiments also apply to other innovative or exploratory programs. Such experiments usually defy the detailed planning, programming, scheduling and evaluation required by international assistance organizations. Indeed, the application of control-oriented planning and management techniques may constrain exploration and establish unrealistic expectations that can lead to false impressions of failure. Because they proceed by trial and error, the course of experimental projects is difficult to predict, let alone control. The development of high-yielding seed varieties in the Puebla Project resulted from just such a pragmatic trial and error methodology. It fell far short of the requirements of a scientifically designed approach or a well-programmed effort. "We never waited for perfection in varieties or methods but used the best available each year and modified them as further improvements came to hand," notes Nobel Prize winning plant geneticist Norman Borlaug (quoted in Poats, 1972: 23), whose team discovered the miracle wheat strains. "This simple principle is too often disregarded by scientific perfectionists who spend a lifetime searching for the unattainable in biological perfection and consequently during a lifetime of frustration contribute nothing to increasing food production."

The decision about how long to run experimental projects can be crucial to their success. Problems have arisen in experimental family planning projects that have been either too long or too short in duration. "Short-run experiments may appear successful because the novelty of their approach guarantees a certain level of impact and because they satisfy the demands of a particular market," Cuca and Pierce (1977: 7) point out. "This success, however, may be short run." But long experiments are difficult to sustain politically. The more social and economic changes that affect the program or area in which experiments are being done, the more difficult it becomes to determine their impacts.

Because experimental projects are often small-scale, they usually require less financial investment than large production projects. But they usually need a substantial amount of scarce professional talent. Personnel recruitment and selection is crucial. Experimental projects require people with an ability to provide creative insights as well as technical knowledge. Highly specialized professionals such as physicians, agronomists, chemists, engineers or managers may be needed to deal with technical problems, but there is also a need for participation by beneficiaries in designing and operating them. The success of the Comilla Project in Bangladesh has been attributed to the ability of staff to learn the most effective means of designing small-scale agricultural and rural development projects from villagers. "The system was developed through a series of trials and errors which involved gathering as much information from the villagers as possible," Choldin (1969: 485) observed. The staff used flexible, pragmatic approaches "to work out methods through interaction with the village clients rather than starting work with preconceived solutions in the form of large-scale plans". A study of small-scale agricultural projects in Latin America and Africa concluded that farmers can play important roles in experimental projects by generating ideas and identifying useful activities, testing the applicability of new methods or techniques and adapting them to local conditions (Morss et al., 1975).

Organizational arrangements must also be given careful attention. Although ideas for experimental projects may be identified, financed and supported by government agencies, they must often be carried out by autonomous or private organizations, such as agricultural experiment stations, industrial research institutes, universities or voluntary groups with special characteristics. If a project is carried out by an operating agency of the government, the staff should be segregated in a project management unit or research and development division, and relieved of routine responsibilities. There are a number of reasons for segregating the staff of experimental projects. First, they usually need an extraordinary amount of flexibility, time to explore widely, and the freedom to make mistakes, which often are not available in bureaucracies that value routinization, expeditious action, standardization and conformity. Second, experiments frequently require special equipment, facilities, supplies and staff with unusual skills, and can be severely hampered by inordinate delays in obtaining them. Third, experiments usually require careful attention to a few special activities that would either compete with or disrupt normal administrative tasks. Finally, there is a danger that experimental projects will be assigned to inappropriate or inadequately trained personnel, or that those who are adequately skilled will resent the additional duties. In the SRDP, for example, junior field staff of some government agencies who were assigned to carry out experimental agricultural development projects complained bitterly (IDS, 1972), and often simply ignored the additional work. In other cases, they merely relabeled their regular duties as "SRDP experiments" to avoid taking on additional responsibilities.

Although the managers of experimental projects are often segregated in special organizations, they need the cooperation of other public agencies. But Cohen (1979) found in his review of integrated rural development projects that cooperation from other organizations is difficult to obtain unless the experimental projects are likely to provide some technical or administrative benefits for them. Thus, the way in which experimental projects are initially described and publicized can have a strong political affect on their future and on the ability of their managers to elicit support and cooperation of other organizations.

Experimental projects need some protection in their early stages from political pressures to terminate them because of mistakes or to replicate them too quickly when they show signs of success. Political leaders are often impatient with experiments, preferring direct action and visible results. Unless experimental projects have strong political and administrative support and a sheltered budget or source of funding, they may be prematurely ended if politicians think that they are progressing too slowly or if they yield results that displease government leaders or powerful vested interests. Political pressures to transform them prematurely into pilot, demonstration or production projects are equally dangerous.

PILOT PROJECTS

Pilot projects can perform a number of important functions: they can test the applicability of innovations in places with conditions similar to those under which experiments were performed; they can test the feasibility and acceptability of innovations in new environments; and they can extend an innovation's range of proven feasibility beyond the experimental stage. They may also serve as small-scale prototypes of larger-scale facilities and test the market for goods and services to be produced by proposed projects. In Mexico, for example, UNDP (1973a) assistance was used to establish a pilot plant to process seaweed and to test the uses of this protein in human nutrition and livestock feed. The pilot project obtained engineering data on commercial production requirements while the acceptability of seaweed in poultry feeds and human diet was being tested. In other countries family planning programs have used pilot projects to determine the costs, effectiveness, political acceptability, operational feasibility and potential impacts of various birth control techniques in different communities (Cuca and Pierce, 1977).

Care must be taken during the transformation from experimental to pilot projects not to use too many foreign personnel or too much imported equipment. Pyle (1980) concluded from his studies of the

Poshak health and nutrition project in India that if this is done local staff may not be able to continue or expand the project on their own. Evaluations (Cuca and Pierce, 1977: 7) of World Bank sponsored family planning programs found that if a pilot scheme is to be replicated, "then it is sensible to limit its resource requirements to those that would be available in the context of the regular program." SRDP projects in Kenya, for example, were modified as they passed from experimental to pilot phases. Financial resources, skilled personnel, foreign experts, supplies and equipment were gradually reduced, modified or eliminated during pilot tests until the prototypes used only those resources normally found in the pilot areas.

In other cases, new resources are needed to adapt experimental projects or to adjust pilot schemes during implementation. An evaluation (Morss et al., 1975) of small-scale agricultural projects in Africa and Latin America found that in adapting integrated rural development activities attention must be given to: (1) the appropriateness of farm size to the proposed technological packages; (2) physical constraints or limitations in the pilot areas; (3) cost of inputs to the farmer and effects on profit conditions; (4) the reliability of service and technology delivery systems in rural areas; (5) the levels of technological complexity in relationship to the farmer's educational background, level of literacy and skills; (6) labor requirements of the new technologies and labor availability; (7) marketing problems and demand for the goods that would be produced with the new techniques; and (8) the amount of risk to the users in adapting the innovations. Care must be taken especially in evaluating the preconditions for successful adaptation of foreign technology.

Because they must be adapted to many different environments, pilot projects may require more financial investment than experiments. As with experiments, it is useful to provide pilot schemes with a stable and secure source of financing to protect them from the political vagaries of the budgeting process, especially if some initial trials prove unsuccessful.

In pilot projects, the acceptability and usefulness of innovations are paramount issues. The SRDP project in Kenya demonstrated that as long as individual farmers retain control over the allocation of their own resources, the factors most directly determining the acceptance of innovations are profitability, costs of adoption, and the risk involved in using them. Where comprehensive, large-scale or socially disruptive innovations are introduced, administrators and planners must thoroughly prepare the people who will be affected and ensure that they play a meaningful role in the process. In land consolidation and redistribution programs in Latin America even landholders with unproductively small plots refused to cooperate because they were not informed of the project in advance and were not prepared to participate. Because planners announced the projects after they had been fully developed, "camposinos found it almost impossible to visualize such a complete change in the landscape, their homes, work habits, services and agricultural practices," Nelson (1973: 244) reports. "Many of the concepts were completely unknown to them." Planners feared that if the public had been informed, opposition groups would have delayed, altered or obstructed the projects.

In rural areas the success of pilot projects depends on the support of strong leaders who are motivated by community spirit. But motivation is unlikely to be sustained unless local leaders also receive more tangible and visible rewards. The success of Korea's *Saemaul Undong* can be attributed largely to the dedication of Saemaul leaders, who were chosen by villagers, and who served without pay. They organized and prodded villagers to cooperate in self-help projects and mobilized resources within the community. Their effectiveness was due not only to their own leadership traits, but also to their selection by villagers, the training provided by the Saemaul Leaders Training Institute, and the competitive approach used by the government to stimulate village development. Anyone over 20 years old, regardless of education, income, or social status, who was chosen by his neighbors, could become a Saemaul leader. Although these leaders were not paid, a variety of non-monetary rewards were made available to them. One was the prestige attached to local leadership of a program strongly supported by Korea's President Park Chung-Hee, whose personal interest and tireless efforts to recognize and reward effective local leaders sustained the incentive system. Special benefits thus made the burdensome job a sought-after post. Recognition opened the way for some Saemaul leaders to receive administrative positions in the national bureaucracy. A variety of honors and awards was granted by the President. Saemaul leaders received discount rates for official trips, qualified for special loans for personal businesses or local projects and could obtain government aid in educating their children. Moreover, because the Saemaul organizational structure was separate from local government, local leaders had access to governors or ministers who could cut red tape and make quick decisions on local problems or grievances (Kim and Kim, 1977). Later, when political leadership in Korea changed and many of these were withdrawn it became more difficult to find motivated people to serve as Saemaul leaders.

Thus, experience with these and with nonformal education, population planning, community development and small-scale agricultural development projects (Niehoff, 1977) suggests that the following factors must be considered carefully in formulating and implementing pilot projects: (1) the basic knowledge, information and wisdom of rural people concerning their own living conditions, perception of problems, identification of needs, and desirability and practicality of new methods; (2) the specific and unique ecological characteristics of areas into which innovations will be introduced, not only natural and physical conditions but also their relationships in supporting human and animal life; (3) an understanding and respect for the diversity of cultural values and norms found within rural villages and communities, their amenability to change and the degree of control that local people have over the factors that create, maintain and alter those values; (4) cultural traits that shape individual behavior and attitudes toward change; (5) the formal and informal authority relationships within communities into which changes will be introduced; (6) the leadership patterns and channels of cooperation, participation, interaction and communication within the community; (7) attitudes toward risk, achievement and motivational incentives.

In the Comilla project, rural institutions were gradually transformed or new ones were created to establish two-way communications between villagers and staff. Educational and training activities were tailored to meet specific and immediate needs (Rahim, 1977). The use of local organizations in small-scale agricultural pilot projects in Africa and Latin America provided a channel for farmer participation and for maintaining regular communications, promoting and reinforcing behavioral changes, facilitating the delivery of complementary services and mobilizing resources for investment in related or supporting projects (Morss *et al.*, 1975).

In the pilot stages, project planning must be flexible and responsive. Cuca and Pierce (1977: 77) found that in pilot family planning projects "a more fluid design is an asset since it permits modification in response to environmental changes and freedom to manipulate inputs." But careful attention must be given to such factors as selecting appropriate sites, because little useful information can be obtained from pilot activities located in areas that are substantially different from "normal" conditions in a country where pilot projects will be replicated. Experience with employment promotion projects in Nigeria indicates that careful consideration must also be given to selecting and recruiting appropriate participants – those who are willing and able to give the project a fair test and who are able to make use of successful results (Mueller and Zevering, 1969).

Other factors must also be considered in designing pilot projects, not the least of which is adjusting activities during implementation to obtain the support, or avoid the overt opposition, of local government officials, political leaders and vested interest groups. Political hostility can doom a pilot project to failure regardless of its potential technical or economic merits. In the Chilalo Agricultural Development Project (CADU) in Ethiopia, for instance, the inability of project staff to generate political support seriously limited the impact on low-income farmers. Cohen (1974) observed that local political elites either resisted or tried to capitalize on CADU. The central government gave the project little of the support it needed to be effective in implementing land reforms, improving local administration or removing obstacles to local participation. Support came only for those activities that did not threaten the interests of local and central government officials.

Experience with the Ethiopian project also points up another important issue – the need to provide or arrange for complementary and supporting resources. This is especially important in rural areas where the organizations, infrastructure, services and personnel needed to make a pilot project successful are rarely found. Thus, the designers of the Intensive Agricultural Districts Program (IADP) in India, who sought to test the most effective ways of increasing food production and income of small-scale cultivators and to broaden the economic base of rural communities, had to provide nearly all of the essential complementary inputs within a single "package scheme." The integrated packages included not only new seed varieties, fertilizers, pesticides and improved farm implements, but also low-interest credit, price supports, improved marketing structures, irrigation facilities and public works, as well as intensive farm management training. In India, as in many other developing countries, the attempt to test the effects of any single input without the provision of the others would have had an extremely low probability of success (Brown, 1971).

But this finding must be balanced off against another: that although a pilot project aims at testing an integrated package of innovations, administrators and planners should do so incrementally. The number of innovations tested at one time should be limited and well focused. Moris (1981) notes in his study of rural development projects in Africa that multiple innovations are difficult to carry out successfully because they place great strains on limited administrative capacity in developing countries.

All of these factors can contribute to the relatively high cost of pilot projects. But if they are successful their contribution to productive capacity may offset some of the costs. Staff training and exposure to new methods and techniques may be of substantial benefit even if the tests prove inconclusive. If pilot projects change cultural norms or values, diffuse new technologies or methods, or increase the willingness of rural people to consider new ideas, they may well be worth their costs.

Like experimental projects, pilot activities must often be designed to protect their staff from undue political interference or pressure to show quick results. Usually pilot projects perform valuable political functions in developing countries by allowing governments to test new ideas or methods under local conditions without committing national leaders to large-scale, uncertain ventures, the failure of which would threaten their prestige and political support. Through pilot projects, innovative techniques, organizational reforms or "foreign methods" may be tested on a small scale, usually without incurring massive resistance or obstruction by those benefiting from the status quo. "Pilot studies do not engage the prestige of the national bureaucracy," Hapgood (1965: 113) has observed. "If one proves unworkable – and it should be stressed that a high proportion of such experiments will probably fail – it can be abandoned or drastically altered without serious loss of face." Pilot, like experimental, projects must often be segregated in semi-autonomous project management units or conducted by autonomous implementation agencies that can provide sufficient political and administrative protection to allow them to run their course.

DEMONSTRATION PROJECTS

The purpose of a demonstration project is to show that new technologies, methods or programs are better than traditional ones because they increase productivity, lower production costs, raise income or deliver social services more efficiently. Their major objective is to show potential adopters the benefits of employing innovations. Thus, although demonstration projects may evolve from experimental and pilot phases they must be designed especially to advocate the adoption of innovation.

Even as the third phase of an experimental and pilot sequence, high levels of risk attend demonstration projects. At this stage, however, the risk is more evenly shared between project sponsors and intended beneficiaries. For example, if new seed varieties, marketing arrangements or cultivation techniques do not produce the results expected by farmers, they can suffer serious financial setbacks and the reputation of extension agents who convinced them to participate can be permanently damaged.

For these reasons, the success of demonstrations depends on a number of principles that Moris (1981: 123) derived from his review of integrated rural development projects in Africa: (1) they must offer low risks for participants; (2) they must provide visible and substantial benefits at the farm level; (3) they must offer participants regular access to cash incomes; (4) they must assist peasant farmers with meeting recurrent costs after the innovation is introduced; (5) they must avoid expanding welfare services before there is a production base that can yield revenue to pay for them; (6) they must use innovations that are not dependent for their adoption on loan financing in the initial phases; (7) they must consider the long-term effects of technology transfer because these may be quite different from immediate effects; (8) they should not be implemented in a way that by-passes local officials, who will remain long after technicians and managers who initiated the project have moved; and (9) they should build administrative capacity on small and incremental, rather than on large-scale and complex, activities that have a higher probability of succeeding.

Saemaul Undong, for example, was based on the principle that demonstration projects must generate immediate and direct benefits for participants in the form of either improved living conditions or higher income. Without visible and immediate benefits, participation is likely to be weak and those who are persuaded to participate may do so apathetically or be distracted by other activities. The success of South Korea's village development program was due to the emphasis that leaders placed on practical and needed projects. The Saemaul leader training program demonstrated beneficial results through applied methods. Assessments of the program (Republic of Korea, 1980: 90) also underline the fact that "Saemaul training has placed more importance on the presentation of success stories, technical training and field study in advanced areas rather than on the simple presentation of ideology. Through this kind of training program, the spirit of diligence, self-help and cooperation could be nurtured and lots of trials and errors could be excluded in the process."

Demonstration projects can also diffuse innovations transferred from other countries. When technology is transferred, the projects should be tested first in a pilot area and then adapted to local conditions and needs. Demonstration projects for small and medium-scale industrial, agricultural and rural development, as Hapgood (1965) notes, should be profitable, novel and include all of the practices required to support them. Methods and technologies must be acceptable and appealing to beneficiaries as well as to project staff. They must be compatible with existing cultural conditions and simple enough to be used with a minimum level of education. Knowledge, materials and other resources required for adoption must be readily available or easily created, and relatively inexpensive. Hapgood found, as Moris (1981) did later, that if farmers are to assume a larger share of the risks in agricultural demonstration projects that use transferred technology, they must be protected from losses through direct compensation, crop insurance, subsidies, incentives or provision of free inputs. Demonstration projects should have a short pay-off period. The new methods should be available to all individuals and groups who are interested in and capable of replicating them.

Demonstration projects must be located carefully and tailored to local conditions. Those geographical areas or populations with the greatest chance of succeeding should be selected first, and others with less favorable characteristics should be chosen later. The experience with integrated agricultural development projects in India indicates that careful site selection was a crucial factor in promoting new farming methods. Among the criteria used in selecting sites were the existence of a tightly organized and previously successful community development program through which participants could be mobilized and services and inputs delivered to them efficiently; credit, supply and marketing cooperatives through which the projects could be administered; sufficient natural resources and appropriate physical and climatic conditions to promote increased crop yields; the lack of major physical obstacles or land tenure problems that would inhibit or sharply increase the costs of operating the projects; and local leadership willing to try new methods and techniques (Brown, 1971).

The organization of the project is also crucial and procedures for introducing innovations must be carefully devised to overcome initial resistance and to sustain the momentum of early adoption. In nearly every developing country the rural people's distrust of public officials makes them suspicious of projects sponsored by national or local government agencies. Moreover, innovations may be resisted because rural people, having lived with existing conditions all of their lives, do not feel the same urgency for change as project staff. The fear of risk is especially important among those living at subsistence levels because the loss of meagre assets endangers their survival.

Drawing on experience with agricultural development projects in Africa and Latin America, Kulp (1977) suggests a six-step strategy for introducing rural demonstration projects: (1) analyze local conditions to compute the best program for the *average* farm in the area; (2) standardize the program as much as possible, consistent with variations in local conditions, so that adoption will be easier and management more efficient; (3) integrate projects into the economy of the area by convincing as many suitable farmers as possible to adopt the program; (4) saturate the area with promotional activities, even if it means over-promoting the program in the early stages; (5) concentrate initial projects in a limited number of areas to prevent overextension of resources and manpower; and (6) accelerate the program rapidly each year after the success of the project has been effectively demonstrated.

Demonstration projects must be gradually and carefully introduced into rural communities. Experience with rural development projects in Asia suggests that a series of well-tested steps should be followed to introduce innovations and that the beneficiaries must be organized to accept them. Haque *et al.* (1977) argue that the role of the initiator − usually project staff members from outside the community − is crucial. The initiator must help to identify appropriate beneficiary groups and work with them in adapting the project to local needs. When projects are aimed at the poorest groups in a community they must be class-biased and deliberately designed to increase the autonomy, self-reliance and political influence of groups that are usually economically dependent and politically powerless. The beneficiaries must be given sufficient resources to be able to take collective action and "de-linked" from traditional dependencies, especially client−patron relationships. Once demonstration projects have succeeded, linkages must be established with groups in other areas to reinforce change and to allow for lateral transfer of experience. Specially trained cadres − people with technical training and with experience in the methods being demonstrated, who are sincerely interested in working with potential beneficiaries − must be made available to assist in demonstration projects. There is some danger in assigning this work to the staff of regular administrative agencies until the projects are ready for full-scale replication and a service delivery system has been tested.

Changes that occur in the demonstration area must be monitored, both to measure the impact on beneficiaries and to modify the project during implementation. The results of demonstration projects must be observed for some time after they are completed, since conditions for success may change drastically. Green Revolution technology in Asia, for instance, often showed excellent results during pilot and demonstration phases by raising agricultural yields, the income of small-scale farmers and the wages of agricultural laborers. But later the results were disappointing. In many places yields decreased and benefits went mainly to large-scale farmers and wealthy landowners because of changes in the conditions under which the new technologies could be used successfully. Widespread adoption uncovered many technical problems that had not been given sufficient attention in pilot phases. Rising costs of inputs − irrigation equipment, petroleum, fertilizers and pesticides − made them accessible only to wealthy farmers. The methods were often replicated in areas where conditions were entirely inappropriate. (Frankel, 1971; Wade, 1974). Moreover, initial increases in income owing to higher crop yields were later offset by technological displacement of labor and unemployment. Haque and his associates (1977) suggest a number of criteria for evaluating rural development demonstration projects, including: (1) changes in the economic base of the community and in the distribution of economic benefits; (2) changes in attitudes and behavior of beneficiaries as expressed in their increased self-reliance, solidarity, and collective and creative activities, and (3) changes in the ability of villagers to initiate and carry out development projects on their own.

If projects demonstrate the effectiveness of new techniques and promote social change they may be criticized severely by those with vested interests in the status quo. Or, project managers may have difficulty resisting political enthusiasm for premature replication. Careful and incremental adaptation is still important at this stage. Weiss, Waterston and Wilson (1977) point out that "the scale of operations is significant for such demonstration projects . . . because many problems do not become fully apparent until a large-scale operation has been reached. In effect, more of the system is tested in demonstration projects because logistics and support mechanisms, a full range of personnel, and other needs must be met to integrate all of the organizational and physical inputs."

Finally, attention must be given to timely completion of the demonstration project and transition to full-scale production or service delivery. Demonstration projects should be terminated when a "critical mass" of intended beneficiaries have adopted their methods, techniques or outputs. The sponsoring agency's efforts should then focus on transferring the innovation to operating agencies, assisting with full-scale production or service delivery, and transferring personnel resources and knowledge to the operating agencies.

REPLICATION, DISSEMINATION AND SERVICE DELIVERY PROJECTS

The dissemination of tested methods, techniques or programs through replication, full-scale production or service delivery projects is the final stage in an experimental series. The major contribution of these projects is to expand productive and administrative capacity. Basic design problems include those of testing full-scale production processes and technology, developing appropriate and effective delivery and distribution systems, transferring production and delivery systems to agencies that can manage them on a larger scale, and maintaining an adaptive and responsive administrative approach after they are transferred. Appropriate scheduling, programming and coordination mechanisms must be used to ensure efficient, economical and reliable production and distribution of goods and services. "In the production stage and even in some of the larger demonstration projects," Weiss, Waterston and Wilson (1977: 101) note, "an additional need has been the quality of entrepreneurship, of working with and exhorting and coordinating the multiple organizations to achieve production-oriented goals."

Undoubtedly, the most difficult problem at this stage is transferring experimental, pilot or demonstration projects to large-scale bureaucracies. Pyle (1980: 123) notes that "corpses of pilot projects, particularly in the social sectors, litter the development field." He concludes from his assessment of the Poshak project in India that careful attention must be given in the earliest stages of pilot and demonstration projects to building political commitment and support among those who will decide about their expansion and replication. The base of support must be broadened quickly when positive results first appear and the interest of other government agencies must be attracted to them. "Because pilot projects do not receive much attention, this added support could be very important when it comes time to discuss the scheme's long-term future," Pyle (1980: 143) argues. "Aggressive public relations efforts during the field work are a necessary part of the pilot project's life if eventual adoption is an objective."

Even when pilot and demonstration projects have been recognized as successful, attempts may be made at the end of the experimental phase to absorb them into the bureaucracy and administer them in conventional style. They are also particularly vulnerable at that point to political attacks that could lead to their abandonment or termination. India's highly successful pilot and demonstration projects in community development during the 1950s and 1960s, for example, were never effectively replicated. Sussman (1980: 115) notes that when the time came for a decision about their replication, "the change to a national scale raised problems different from those of a project of limited size and duration." Indian leaders were required to make new, more extensive and potentially threatening commitments. "Choices on national priorities involve heavy outlays of capital resources and expenditures. The question that decision-makers may therefore find themselves asking is not, What is the *best* way of doing community development? but, What is the most politically and bureaucratically *feasible* way to do community development?" In India political pressures to extend the program's coverage led officials to disregard the well-managed, responsive, adaptive and innovative approaches that had evolved from the pilot and demonstration phases and to absorb community development activities into the national extension service, which was organized hierarchically and managed so rigidly that it was nearly impossible to carry them on in an adaptive and responsive manner. From the experience with India's community development program, Sussman (1980: 121) cogently concludes

> that the calculus involved in the development of a national program is complex and depends even more on political and bureaucratic perspectives than it does on what is learned in the field trial, the pilot project or the demonstration project. Thus, we might expect in other cases that the pilot project might well *not* be adopted as a model for the national program unless its political utility and feasibility can be demonstrated to be the most attractive alternative to decision-makers.

The greatest problem of transforming experimental, pilot and demonstration projects into larger-scale production or service delivery programs is the assumption that they can be transferred to all parts of a country without further testing or adaptation and that they can be managed by conventional procedures. But all development projects are somewhat experimental, and even seemingly routine replications of thoroughly tested technology or construction methods often meet unanticipated difficulties when transferred from one cultural setting to another, from specialized project units to regular operating agencies, or from the demonstration stage to full-scale production.

Organizational problems become paramount, for even when previous experimental activities have resolved technical and administrative uncertainties, new problems tend to arise simply with expansion of scale. Although pilot and demonstration projects in Comilla, Bangladesh proved to be highly successful under the leadership of the Academy for Rural Development, for example, new operational problems arose when prototypes were transformed into a nationwide Integrated Rural Development Program (IRDP). "In the expanded setting of the national program, those problems have been greatly magnified," one official of the Academy (Rahim, 1977: 67) observed. "The three main Ministries and their affiliated departments – Agriculture, Rural Development and Education – seem to be in constant conflict over the allocation of funds, jurisdiction and sharing of responsibilities and rewards. Scarcity of funds and other resources is another serious constraint. The inevitable result of these problems is that the IRDP has been threatened by bureaucratic centralization at the national level and poor implementation at the rural level."

The diffusion of new agricultural technologies has been severely hampered in developing countries by the difficulty of organizing extension services appropriately and of recruiting and motivating extension agents. Demands made on their time by bureaucratic procedures, paperwork requirements, or the remoteness of headquarters from the farms; the lack of adequate equipment and supplies; the unwillingness of agents to work closely with peasants and small-scale farmers are common problems. Agents often come from urban areas and have limited knowledge of agriculture. Their low level of rapport with and respect for their clients creates mutual distrust and hostility. Attitudes of superiority and paternalistic behavior quickly reduce agents' effectiveness. Their unwillingness to live in rural areas or to spend sufficient time with farmers makes it difficult to gain their clients' respect or to learn of their unique problems and needs. Moreover, departments of agriculture often fail to provide the resources needed by farmers to apply new technologies effectively, further alienating the extension agents from their clientele (Trapman, 1974; Leonard, 1977; Heginbotham, 1975).

The choice of organization to carry out production or service delivery projects is crucial. A variety of organizational arrangements can be used, but experience suggests that no single arrangement is universally effective. Each form has its advantages and limitations, depending on the administrative, cultural and political conditions under which the projects must be implemented.

Among the organizational alternatives currently used to implement projects are (Rondinelli, 1979):

1 an existing department or ministry, in which the project is implemented as part of an ongoing program without creating a distinct project management unit;
2 a distinct project management unit within an existing government ministry, that is given all of the resources needed to implement the project or provided with functional support from specialized departments in a matrix arrangement;
3 an autonomous implementation unit outside of the regular government operating structure, with sufficient resources and authority to implement the project, independent sources of revenue, recruiting, hiring and training capability, the ability to pay higher salaries and provide greater amenities than regular civil service agencies and the authority to contract for foreign technical and financial assistance;
4 a decentralized field unit reporting to a central government agency, usually created to undertake functionally specialized or regional development projects that cannot be implemented directly by a central government ministry;

5   an interagency coordinating committee, which attempts to integrate the resources of a variety of ministries, subordinate units of government, and private organizations or groups, with staff seconded from one or more of the ministries for temporary duty;

6   a private contractor or production firm that undertakes construction and operation of the project under government supervision, or on a "turnkey" basis, whereby a private firm constructs the project and then turns it over to a government agency for operation;

7   a lower level of government through devolution of project management functions to provincial, state or local units, with or without central government supervision and monitoring; and

8   joint ventures in which government and private firms share responsibility for the construction, operation and delivery of goods and services, and maintenance of the project, with duties, powers and responsibilities of each party clearly delineated.

Some governments and international aid agencies prefer to assign projects to existing organizations, integrating them with ongoing programs to build administrative capacity. Others insist on creating autonomous implementation units for each project to overcome administrative weaknesses. This approach also hedges against risk by requiring a single organization to have sufficient resources to carry out the project and to shelter the staff from other administrative duties (Rondinelli and Ruddle, 1977).

Regardless of the type of organization used to implement development activities, Moris (1981: 24) has found that certain principles are essential for adaptive and responsive administration. He observes that (1) the success of a project depends ultimately on finding managers who are dedicated and committed to its goals and purposes and who are given discretion in making choices as the need arises during implementation; (2) supervision procedures should be kept simple and the chain of command kept short; (3) the project should be kept under the control of a single organization, but contacts should be maintained with others that can support and promote its activities; (4) staff should be recruited from among qualified people who have served in the area where the project will be located; (5) staff should work through local officials when contacting local residents, and those who work directly with beneficiaries should be well trained, supervised and supported; (6) staff, consultants and contractors should be chosen on the basis of their past performance; (7) political constraints should be taken seriously and, when it is possible, the priorities of politicians who can affect the success of the project should be accommodated; (8) resources and attention should be focused on only one or two major activities at a time, starting small and aiming at complete success with each step of expansion; (9) subordinates should be given as much experience as possible and be allowed occasionally to stand in for experienced leaders in order to create a pool of future leaders who can carry on the project's activities.

Although attempts should be made to standardize and institutionalize as many tasks as possible during replication and dissemination, care must be taken to maintain an adaptive and responsive approach to administration. Standardization is possible, but often risky. Nelson (1973: 324) found from his study of Latin American land development projects, for instance, that the "quantity and quality of extension agents are aspects of colonization project design about which it is almost impossible to set ground rules. . . . No standard basis can be established to justify a ratio of 1:100 over 1:1,000." Where professionals are scarce or replication depends on high levels of participation it may be desirable to use local paraprofessionals or to devolve administrative responsibilities directly to local groups. Experience with creating and using small-farmer organizations for implementing agricultural development and credit projects in Ecuador and Honduras has shown that they are most effective when (1) they are organized to accomplish specific and tangible goals; (2) they begin with a single achievable task rather than multiple objectives; (3) tasks can be carried out with the skills farmers currently possess; (4) cooperation is required to accomplish the task and cannot be done by individuals working alone; and (5) the groups are small and not closely related to or dependent on others (Tendler, 1976). In initial stages of replication attention should be focused on building or strengthening local organizational capability.

Building administrative capacity often requires changes in traditional practices and behavior. As noted earlier, however, international assistance agencies have not been successful in using incentives or penalties to promote behavioral changes. Tendler (1976) suggests a number of ways that they can design projects more effectively. First, more attention must be paid to ensuring that preconditions are met before loan or grant funds are dispersed. If governments are not willing to make changes before receiving funds, it is unlikely that they will do so afterward. Moreover, disbursement could be made in installments, based on easily measured or observable indicators of progress. Incentives that are related to the pace or size of disbursements can be used to reward desired behavior. Further, the institutions receiving assistance should be required to match or contribute local funds, so that the costs of failure become higher for the government. Less reliance should be placed on grants, and those that are made should contain a pay-back requirement if government agencies fail to make changes in practices or procedures required to achieve project goals. Parts of loans should be forgiven if greater than expected progress is achieved. Finally, international agencies must be more willing to evaluate projects so that they can be terminated when recipients refuse to make changes or conform to project agreements. Institutions failing to fulfill mutually agreed-upon conditions should be ineligible for financial assistance for a specified period of time (Tendler, 1976). The changes required of bureaucracies, however, cannot be so foreign to their customs and traditions that they inhibit acceptance or impose practices that obstruct adaptive administration. Special attention must also be given to identifying and using informal methods of decision-making and interaction. Coordination and cooperation in most developing nations are achieved not by command but through informal, personal networks of interaction. They usually depend on complex patron–client and personal obligation and exchange relationships that cannot, and probably should not, be displaced quickly with formal administrative or organizational mechanisms. Grindle (1977: 40) notes that, in Mexico, bureaucratic "informal exchange networks develop because they are perceived to be, and are in fact, an efficient and effective means of goal attainment." These informal networks of personal exchange and obligation extend throughout the bureaucracy:

> In Mexico, exchange relationships bind public officials from various institutions together for the pursuit of policy goals: they serve to connect individuals within one agency for defense against the functional encroachments of another; they tie the bureaucratic elite to the political chiefs and make possible intragovernmental problem solving; and the manner in which they link the nationally oriented regional elite to the bureaucratic center is useful in understanding problems of policy implementation.

Although more detailed programming is possible after pilot and demonstration stages, over-emphasis on technical efficiency and heavy reliance on detailed programming, scheduling and networking techniques may lead administrators to overlook broader political issues. And although political threats to the survival of projects may be less severe in this stage than in experimental, pilot and demonstration phases, replication and production projects face potential problems arising from political apathy and administrative inefficiency that can seriously obstruct their implementation.

Experience also suggests that development administrators not only should have appropriate technical and managerial skills, but also must provide strong leadership, especially in mobilizing resources, interacting politically with other leaders, motivating staff, clients and sponsors, building a network of organizational support, and solving problems creatively. Agricultural production projects in Nepal were ineffective during the 1960s because they were administered bureaucratically, whereas similar projects in the Philippines were more successful because they were assigned to energetic, determined, persuasive and motivated leaders. Land development in Sri Lanka was bogged down in delays and red tape and eventually failed for the lack of responsive leadership, while similar projects in Malaysia were strongly guided and directed by men who were widely regarded as honest, intelligent and committed (Vepa, 1977).

Political commitment and leadership from higher level authorities are also crucial. The lackluster experience with large-scale public housing projects in Hong Kong has been attributed to bureaucratic strangulation, whereas such projects in Singapore received international acclaim. The success of Singapore's projects resulted primarily from the "highly effective leadership of a young prime minister, Lee Kuan Yew, for whom no detail was too small to be considered" (Vepa, 1977: 171). In Malaysia rural development projects were efficiently administered through the red book and operations room systems, which was vigorously promoted by Prime Minister Tun Abdul Razak. For several years during the 1960s, Esman (1977: 225) notes, "Tun Razak made this system work by exhaustive pressure – surprise visits to state and district operations rooms and dramatic intervention on the spot. He exhorted officers to greater effort, to speed up performance, to work together, to concentrate on development activities, and he achieved results in speeding up action and demonstrating to rural Malays the government's concern for their welfare." But when he turned his attention to other matters, the once effective techniques were frozen in bureaucratic procedures; the impacts of the projects were dissipated and progress ground slowly to a halt. Without strong administrative and political support, conventional methods of planning and management are inadequate to control the course of implementation and the adaptive and responsive approaches to administration that have been described in this chapter are difficult to introduce and sustain.

5

Reorienting development administration: principles, problems and opportunities

Applying the principles of adaptive, learning-based administration depends on changing the perceptions of planners, administrators and policy-makers about the nature of development and of social problem-solving. Conventional approaches to development administration are based on inaccurate or inappropriate assumptions about the process of development and the tasks of development planning, the conditions under which change is possible and the means through which it occurs in developing societies.[1]

Development administration theory of the 1950s and 1960s was reflected in two somewhat different but not mutually exclusive approaches. One group of development administration theories, which Siffin (1977) has labeled "tool oriented," contended that policy implementation could be improved in developing nations through the transfer of administrative procedures and techniques from industrial countries, and especially from the United States, Britain and France. The other – advanced by political development theorists and administrative reformers – argued that political processes and administrative structures had to be thoroughly transformed and modernized before governments in developing countries could achieve economic and social progress.

Those who believed that administrative capacity in developing countries could be expanded by transferring procedures and techniques from industrial nations followed the Weberian model. They attempted to establish within developing countries administrative procedures that were "rational" and politically impartial. Advocates of this approach insisted that development administration was concerned with the "technical procedures and organizational arrangements by which a government achieves movement toward development goals" (Katz, 1970: 120) and was concerned with the methods used by governments to attain their development objectives through the implementation of national plans and policies (Riggs, 1970). The United Nations' *Handbook of Public Administration* (1961) embodied the tool-oriented approach and prescribed the hierarchical organization of bureaucracies, creation of politically impartial civil services in the British tradition, the adoption of Western personnel administration systems in which appointment and promotion were to be based on skill and merit, the transfer of many service functions to public enterprises, creation of program budgeting systems, and the training of top- and middle-level administrators in the techniques of modern management.

Political modernizers, on the other hand, believed that the transfer of administrative procedures and techniques from Western democracies, although necessary, was not sufficient. They viewed development administration as "social engineering," and national governments as the prime movers of social change. Landau (1970: 75) defined development administration as a "directive and directional process which is intended to make things happen in a certain way over intervals of time;" others perceived of it as a means of improving the capacities of governments to deal with problems created by modernization and change (Lee, 1970; Spengler, 1963). Development administration would be the instrument for transforming traditional societies. Unless the entire political system was reformed and modernized, governments of developing nations could not adequately direct and control social and economic progress.

Traditional approaches to development administration came under heavy criticism during the 1970s. Siffin (1977) concisely summarized the weaknesses of the tool-oriented approach: in attempting to create rational, politically impartial, efficient and democratic administrative systems it promoted Western values that were often inappropriate or irrelevant in other societies. It was assumed that complex social problems could be solved with modern administrative techniques. But in many countries the transfer of Western methods simply introduced predetermined solutions and inhibited development of analytical skills that would enable planners and administrators to deal with unique indigenous problems as they arose. Moreover, the tools were transferred from well-structured institutions in industrial societies to loosely organized governments in the developing world, where they could not work as effectively. Indeed many procedures and techniques, such as program budgeting and systems analysis, were transferred from industrial nations before their effectiveness had been proven. But in countries where the techniques took hold they created powerful technocratic classes that were often out of touch with the problems and needs of their own people, and especially those of the rural poor. Finally, the tools of Western administration were concerned primarily with maintenance functions and thus did little to improve government's capacity to promote development.

Similar criticisms have been made of political modernization theories. They were ethnocentric and based on philosophies and values that often rendered them useless or perverse in developing nations. Pye (1965) points out that theory never yielded a concise definition of political development. It was variously defined as creating political prerequisites for industrialization, creating government institutions with characteristics similar to those found in European states, reforming legal and administrative structures in the American or British tradition, mass mobilization and participation in political processes, creating procedures for orderly political succession, and sharing power and authority democratically.

Perhaps the most serious shortcoming of traditional approaches to development administration, however, was that their prescriptions for modernizing administrative procedures, institutions and structures ignored the fact that a wide variety of other factors condition the amount of change that can be promoted in developing countries. This is illustrated quite clearly when the experience of developing nations with implementing administrative reform programs is examined and the obstacles are identified. Recent attempts by governments in Tanzania, Kenya and the Sudan, for example, to decentralize development administration and planning functions, strengthen local institutions and reorganize the political structure to attain more equitable economic growth and extend participation to rural people, underline the complexity of policy implementation (Rondinelli, 1981; 1981a; 1983). Experiences in those countries indicate that essential political, economic and social preconditions must be established before reorganization becomes feasible. Successful implementation of decentralization programs in East Africa required far more than simply declaring a policy of "bottom-up" decision-making, reorganizing the administrative structure and creating new local or district planning procedures. Both local and central government officials must be committed to the philosophy of decentralization and to popular participation in decision-making. Widespread political support must be generated among national political leaders for transferring planning, decision-making and managerial authority to field agencies of national ministries and to lower levels of administration. Support must also be created among officials in the central bureaucracy and their technical and administrative capacity to facilitate and guide local administrative units must be expanded. Functions must be allocated to local units incrementally, based on their capacity to meet performance criteria. The success of decentralization depends on increasing the flow of resources to local levels through intergovernmental fiscal transfers or by assisting localities to raise their own revenues. Moreover, the disappointing results of organizational reforms in East Africa illustrate the importance of creating environmental conditions that are more conducive to decentralized planning and administration. Local administrative units and governments need a network of local institutions to support them in carrying out development activities. Provisions must be made for extending physical infrastructure, transport and communications linkages in areas where decentralization is to be promoted and for distributing services and facilities that will enable local residents to participate effectively in local decision-making. Although the policies pursued in East Africa sought to attain quite radical changes, they were based on traditional assumptions of development administration: that reform of administrative procedures, institutions and structures alone could promote social and economic change. Failure to incorporate into plans and policies those economic, social, cultural and physical factors that shape the society in which reforms must be implemented, created obstacles to achieving government objectives.

The Weberian model of organization has been especially inappropriate for developing countries because it overlooked or ignored the high level of uncertainty attending the implementation of development policies. It was primarily modeled on European government systems in which routine and standardized administrative procedures were suited to solving marginal and easily identified problems. But in developing countries the only certainty is that the course of development programs and projects is uncertain. Solving one aspect of a problem or one set of problems merely uncovers or creates new ones, many of which cannot be anticipated and therefore cannot be dealt with through routine and standardized administrative procedures. "Success in one sphere – e.g., the introduction of a new technology like cattle dipping – will lead to new constellations of problems (marketing efficiency, input supply, corruption, etc.) present all along but masked by the initial difficulty," Moris (1981: 123) concluded from his review of rural development projects in Africa. "Programs that have as their goal human betterment should anticipate that the focus of program effort will have to change over time, as one problem after another is dealt with." The difficulty of formulating policies and projects comprehensively, and managing them systematically, is that usually hidden obstacles and unanticipated problems "cannot be specified in advance, and so will not be listed within the initial scope of program activities."

Many of the difficulties with conventional planning and administration can be overcome only by reorienting administrative practices and procedures and by changing the perceptions of those involved in development about effective planning and implementation. The challenge to development administrators is of finding more appropriate ways of dealing with the inevitable uncertainty and complexity of development problems. Among the changes that must be made are: adjusting planning procedures and methods of administration to the processes of political interaction through which policies are actually made and carried out; adopting a learning-based approach to planning and administration in order to cope with uncertainty and complexity; building widespread and appropriate forms of administrative capacity within developing societies; decentralizing to the appropriate level authority for planning and administering development activities; simplifying analysis and management procedures; encouraging rather than suppressing or punishing error detection and correction; and creating greater flexibility for development administrators to manage complex and uncertain ventures by offering incentives for innovation, risk-taking and learning. Together, these principles form an alternative approach to development management: a process of adaptive administration.

ADJUSTING PLANNING AND ADMINISTRATIVE PROCEDURES TO THE POLITICAL ENVIRONMENT OF PUBLIC POLICY-MAKING

Ultimately, all plans are political statements and all attempts to implement them are political acts. The pretension that planners and administrators are politically objective or neutral is naive. The belief that politics is beyond the scope of development administration usually reduces planners and administrators to a politically ineffective advisory role in which plans are produced but not advocated and little attempt is made to intervene in the political process to mobilize support for them. The illusion that they are "above politics" sometimes leads planners and administrators to rely predominantly or exclusively on control-oriented approaches that are irrelevant or perverse. The politics of development planning and implementation has been given relatively little attention in development theory and this may explain, in part, its failure to deal explicitly with its political dimensions.

Often it is assumed that because most developing countries do not have democratic or participative political systems that decisions are made by a ruling elite without conflict or political interaction, and that they are carried out dutifully by bureaucrats in the lower levels of the administrative hierarchy. Recent studies of the politics of development planning and administration indicate, however, that a great deal of political conflict and interaction attend decision-making and implementation, even in authoritarian political systems. Moreover, they indicate that comprehensive planning and central control of development projects and programs are rarely effective in situations where decisions are made and implemented, not by command, but through the interaction of groups with different interests, objectives, sources of power and capacities to undermine or block the action of others.

The degree to which political interaction affects development decisions at national and local levels is explored in Grindle's studies (1977: 18–19) of policy-making in Latin America, where elite groups and national bureaucracies dominate the political process, but where, she argues, "the factions, patron–client linkages, ethnic ties and personal coalitions that are often the basis of political activity are well suited to making individualized demands on the bureaucratic apparatus for the allocation of goods and services." In a case history of an urban renewal and market reform project in Cali, Colombia, Bromley (1981: 14) notes how decisions often evolve, not from the plans of technical experts, but from political interaction among conflicting interest groups. The participants act "frequently, and sometimes necessarily, on the basis of incomplete or incorrect information, with information and motives often being deliberately hidden or distorted in the quest for a broad base of support." Rather than seeking to make and follow deliberate, well-researched, and comprehensive plans for development projects, participants allow their own actions to be shaped by the interaction of competing interest groups, by preceding and unfolding events, by external forces and by unpredictable reactions of private and government organizations during the course of the conflict.

Quick's (1980: 57) analysis of rural development programs in Zambia also underlines the importance of interaction among political elites, government agencies and rural interest groups in formulating and implementing development policies. He too emphasizes the inability of participants, and especially government agencies, to make and carry out detailed rational plans, arguing that "agencies with multiple, ambiguous and immeasurable goals find it difficult to develop technically rational solutions to the problems of implementation. They have no logical way of setting priorities or organizing routines." If faced with the choice between having to do systematic planning and doing nothing, they will avoid taking action. If political pressures make the latter alternative impossible, they will fall back on political criteria for decision-making and, as Quick (1980: 57) observed in Zambia, "such criteria demand a simplification of the agency's operational goal structure, eliminating many of the nonmeasurable or long-run goals and focusing attention exclusively on activity that will yield short-run, measurable results."

Comprehensiveness, consistency, a long-range view and cost-effectiveness – the criteria by which planners supposedly forge their proposals for development – are heavily discounted by bureaucratic agencies under pressure to act quickly. As Quick perceptively concludes from the cases in Zambia, "immediate results have a political utility for the organization regardless of the contribution that such activity makes to the long-run success of its program."

When development activities are funded by international agencies, the organizational environment of decision-making becomes more complex and uncertain, and political interaction becomes more intense. Gordenker (1976: 11–12) observes that "because economic development is the very stuff of politics – the kernel of crucial decisions – in many less-developed countries the work of international organizations necessarily and increasingly touches on controversial and delicate national issues." The advice offered to governments in developing countries by the staff or consultants of international agencies can change the balance of political power among interest groups, expand or constrain the access of various groups to centers of decision-making, alter the government's development priorities or generate social changes with undesired political impacts. "To make recommendations about the organization of an educational system, to arm a minister of transport with arguments for extending a road network that competes for capital funds with a weapons-seeking defense ministry, to urge population control on people who for the first time in the memory of the oldest man enjoy reasonably good health," Gordenker (1976: 12) asserts, "is to be involved in politics."

As a result of their political potency, projects and programs often evolve from a process of political interaction involving one or more international agencies, a variety of national ministries and agencies, private organizations and clientele or beneficiary groups, as well as powerful individuals within and outside of government. Noting that political interaction fundamentally influenced the scope and shape of projects in Malawi, Tanzania and Zambia, Gordenker (1976: 97–8) points out that, at least in the case of United Nations sponsored projects, "giving definition to a request for international aid can lead to considerable friction within and among the organizations of the UN system as well as to divisions of opinion within the recipient government. Intractable disagreements can prevent the submission of a request. Even if a formula can be found, the original idea for the project is likely to undergo marked alteration."

Even organizations such as the World Bank, which are mandated by their policies and procedures to control carefully the conditions under which projects are selected and carried out, have great difficulty achieving their goals without political negotiation and compromise. Observing the Bank's role in funding population projects in developing countries, Crane and Finkle (1981: 538) contend that it "is constrained in its ability to work effectively in the complex political and administrative environment of national population programs by its relations with client ministries and its own project procedures. The presence of numerous other organizations in the population field makes this environment even more complex and introduces additional sources of difficulty and uncertainty for the Bank."

In a complex decision-making environment, in which political commitment and support from powerful groups is a necessary but not sufficient condition for the success of development projects, control-oriented planning and administration is usually neither relevant nor effective. The lessons of past experience suggest that development administration must be more facilitative and that more appropriate methods of intervention in the political process must be used by development planners and administrators to mobilize support for policies, programs and projects.

One important challenge to development administrators is to identify and test procedures and techniques of planning and management that rely less on central control and more on incentives and exchange. This does not mean that governments in developing countries should try to weaken or dismantle central ministries and bureaucracies, but that they should seek to reorient the role of central agencies from one of attempting to dominate and control development projects to one of facilitating and supporting decentralized implementation. In developing countries the resources of a broad range of groups are needed to ensure the success of projects and programs. As Leonard (1977: 213) correctly points out in his study of agricultural administration in Kenya, "in a decentralized administrative structure the center needs to be every bit as strong as in a centralized one, but the reorientation required is one of technical service rather than of hierarchical control."

A variety of methods of intervention and interaction are actually used to influence the outcome of policy conflicts and to shape the content and direction of development policies in developing countries. But because development planning and administration have traditionally been defined as technical, politically neutral and objectively rational activities, these methods are rarely explored in the literature or recognized as being essential instruments in the development process. The methods most often recommended and used by development planners and administrators – central control and coordination – are often the least effective instruments of influence where the political environment allows access to decision-making, or affords the potential for delay, disruption or defeat of policies by special interest groups within and outside of government.

To be more effective, development administrators must explicitly recognize and use a wide variety of methods of influence, including information dissemination, public education, specialized training programs, persuasion and consultation techniques. They require a lower degree of direct intervention in specific policy conflicts but may be more effective in shaping the behavior of participants in the political process than direct control or central coordination. More sophisticated methods of psychological manipulation, modeling and techniques that psychologists call "shaping and reinforcement" are also available to influence behavior through non-coercive means (see Figure 3). Incentives and rewards can often be used more effectively to achieve desired behavior than punishments and threats, which are usually the basis of control-oriented methods of management (Rondinelli, 1975; 1976).

Much more attention must be given to processes of reciprocal exchange, compromise, the trading of promises and threats, formal and informal bargaining and negotiation, mediation, and coalition building in the process of decision-making if development planners and administrators are to become more effective in coping with the complexity and uncertainty of development problems.

INCREASING THE RESPONSIVENESS OF ORGANIZATIONS THROUGH PARTICIPATORY AND MARKET SURROGATE ARRANGEMENTS

One means of improving the responsiveness of bureaucratic organizations is to restructure them to be more sensitive to pressures from their environments and to provide incentives that reinforce and reward staff performance that satisfies the needs of clientele. Another approach is to increase competitive pressures on bureaucracies by introducing market surrogates for institutional development.

Studies of complex organizations in the public and private sectors of both developing and industrialized countries indicate that they must be structured much differently to promote innovation, creativity and responsiveness under conditions of uncertainty than to deliver services in routine and standardized fashion. In unstable and uncertain environments organizations must be responsive to survive. Under these conditions organic rather than mechanistic structures are needed. An organic structure requires (Burns and Stalker, 1961):

1   Breaking organizational activities down into task-oriented subunits rather than specialized abstract subunits;

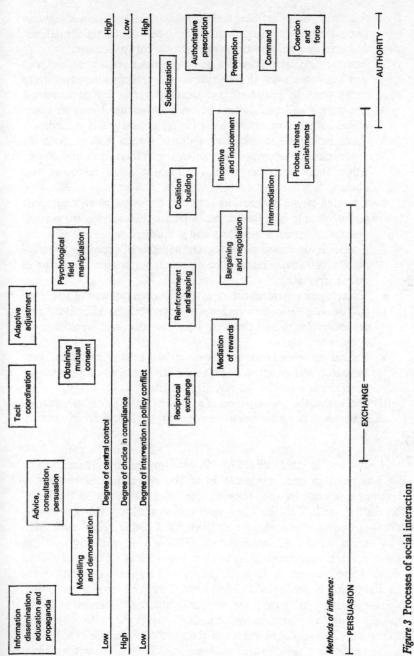

Figure 3 Processes of social interaction

Source: Rondinelli (1976).

2   Adjusting and redefining tasks through the interaction of organizational members rather than allowing them to be rigidly defined and adjusted only by the organization's formal leaders;

3   Encouraging individuals to accept broader responsibilities and commitments than those prescribed by their functional roles rather than defining staff duties exclusively in functional terms;

4   Creating a collegial system of decision-making based on interaction rather than strictly hierarchical authority and control;

5   Recognizing the limited knowledge of formal leaders about the organization's activities and soliciting information and knowledge about activities from the organization's members and clients;

6   Creating lateral communications and consultation arrangements among people in different ranks rather than relying on vertical command between superiors and subordinates;

7   Encouraging decision-making on the basis of exchange of information and advice rather than on top-down process of command and instruction;

8   Creating an environment in which the commitment of staff is to performing tasks and fulfilling responsibilities effectively and responsively rather than to blind loyalty and obedience to superiors;

9   Providing rewards for prestige attached to staff members' performance and expertise in the larger environment rather than for performance within the organization itself; and

10   Increasing the participation of staff and clients in decisions about changes in the organization's missions, goals and functions.

Thomas and Brinkerhoff (1978: 12) confirm the importance of these characteristics in their examination of the experience of responsive development organizations such as the Joint Commission for Rural Reconstruction in Taiwan. They point out, in addition, that it is important to structure tasks so that responsibility and authority are devolved to many units within the organization. This allows authority, policy, initiatives and innovative ideas to flow inward and upward as well as outward and downward. In participatory and responsive organizations the distinction between political and administrative behavior loses much of its meaning: "managers are seen as active contributors to policy making as are all members and clients of the organization." Indeed, clients would have a high degree of access to opportunities for participation in decision-making and management. Such organizations must give equal priority if not more importance to equity as to efficiency and economy.

Moreover, Ickis (1981: 11–12) argues that in a development organiz-ation that seeks to be responsive, the dominant goal must be to facilitate self-determination among its clients or within the community with which it is dealing. The role of a government agency in this case is to provide support for community initiatives and to make available modest amounts of unrestricted resources. Beneficiaries are seen as independent initiators of activities. Ickis insists that a primary assumption of a responsive organization is that, if left to their own devices and provided with basic support, the beneficiaries can and will identify and act on their own needs appropriately. The supporting agency will be highly decentralized, staffed with generalists and its primary units will be organized in such a way as to allow staff to interact directly with the community. Communications will be carried out primarily through personal contact. The basic indicator of performance would be the number of beneficiaries participating in community-controlled develop-ment activities.

Often a less costly and more expedient alternative to organizational reform is to change the external environment of an agency to make it more competitive and to reduce the organization's dominant or mon-opoly power over its clients. Lamb (1982) has suggested a number of ways this can be done. One is by encouraging *direct competition*, that is, allowing or encouraging more public institutions or private and volun-tary organizations to perform specified development functions or to offer goods and services previously provided by only one or a few public agencies. Often competition can be encouraged through licensing, regulation, de-regulation or subsidization. In some developing countries traditional institutions as well as government agencies are used to provide services in rural areas. Others sub-contract to private firms in order to supplement or enhance the capacity of public agencies. Govern-ments often share responsibilities with private firms or allow public enterprises to provide services in order to introduce competition in the public sector.

Another market surrogate for institutional development is to *actively market government services*, that is, to make consumer preferences more influential in decisions about service provision and delivery. Lamb (1982: 4) argues that government agencies would be required to "provide and market a convenient 'shelf' of information and services, in contrast to a fixed or predetermined 'package' from which users could select their desired mix. This might apply to productive services (e.g., agricultural inputs and extension), to social services (e.g., literacy, health, family planning) or to a combination of the two plus other public and private services." Such an approach would require the creation of an appropriate structure for service delivery, with the kinds of characteristics that will be described later in this chapter.

A third market surrogate involves *organizing recipients, users and suppliers* so that external constituencies can bring pressure on public agencies to be more effective and responsive in performing their tasks. Unofficial or voluntary organizations can also provide goods and services on a low-cost, self-help basis, thereby lessening clients' dependence on a single public agency. The organization of recipients, users and suppliers creates a system of countervailing power that provides channels of interaction between client and agency.

Finally, use of *performance agreements*, in which functions are contracted or delegated to nongovernment agencies, is another means of introducing market surrogates in the public sector. Public enterprises or private organizations would be given contractual responsibilities for performing functions, providing services or producing goods for as long as they perform their responsibilities effectively and responsively. Changes could be made in the agreements to ensure continued effectiveness and responsiveness without initiating massive bureaucratic reorganizations that could easily be opposed by entrenched civil servants.

Eventually, making the environment of public agencies more competitive would require them to reorganize internally along the lines suggested earlier. Creating competition would provide clients with alternative sources of obtaining goods and services and give them bargaining power that would allow them to obtain more responsive and effective treatment by public agencies.

ADOPTING A LEARNING-BASED APPROACH TO PLANNING AND ADMINISTRATION

The application of adaptive administration, as noted in chapter 1, requires planners and administrators to view social problem-solving as an incremental process of social interaction, trial and error, successive approximation and social learning. Such an approach requires an institutional context quite different from that of Weberian bureaucracies. The recognition of these needs led in the 1970s to the institution-building approach to development administration. The theory of institution-building was based on the premise that their poor record of implementing development policies was the result of developing country governments' inability to perform essential development functions. Siffin (1977: 59) argued that "the essence of development is not to maintain, but to create effectively. . . . Doing this means, among other things, marshalling substantial amounts of knowledge about organizational design and the effects of alternative organizational arrangements." Thompson (1964) insisted that Weberian models of bureaucracy were inappropriate for performing the innovative and creative tasks required of development administration, and that development administrators needed institutions that provided an atmosphere conducive to innovation. Both tool-oriented and administrative reform approaches sought to strengthen the central government's control over development. But because policies change rapidly in developing countries, Thompson argued that they were not susceptible to central direction. He called for institutions in which administrators could solve problems more creatively: non-hierarchical, non-bureaucratic, professional, problem-oriented systems in which communications structures were loose and in which decisions evolved from group interaction.

Esman (1969: 13) defined institution-building as "the planning, structuring, and guidance of new or reconstituted organizations which a) embody changes in values, functions, physical and/or social technologies, b) establish, foster and protect new normative relationships and action patterns, and c) obtain support and complementarity in the environment." Its aim was to create "viable development institutions"; that is, those with the following characteristics: (1) technical capacity – the ability to deliver technical services that are innovative for the society into which they are introduced; (2) normative commitment – the ability to internalize innovative ideas, relationships and practices within the staff of the organization; (3) innovative thrust – the ability of the organization to continue to innovate so that new technologies and behavior patterns will not be "frozen" in their original form; (4) environmental image – the ability of the organization to attain favorable recognition within society and be highly valued or regarded by other organizations; and (5) spread effects – the ability of the organization to get other institutions to adapt the innovative technologies, norms or methods that it has introduced. Institution-building strategy was concerned not only with strengthening the administrative capacity of individual organizations, but also with forging cooperative relationships among them.

Although the institution-building approach recognized the need for an innovative, learning-based style of administration, application was generally limited to central government ministries and to large educational and research institutes. The abstractness of the theory made it difficult to apply in the Third World, and where it was applied it was often considered to be an end in itself. It did not, therefore, address questions of equity and participation or seek to increase the access of the poorest groups to institutional resources. Adaptive administration requires not only more flexible and responsive institutions that can cope with uncertainty and complexity, but also a combination of organizational flexibility with a learning-based process of planning and administration.

Korten (1981: 613) has argued that development planning and administration must be based more on social learning than on scientific management. It must depend less on finding subjectively rational and optimal or "correct" solutions than on discovering useful actions that can ameliorate adverse conditions of individuals and groups who are affected by them and in ways that are acceptable to them. He argues that

> the key to social learning is not analytical method, but organizational process; and the central methodological concern is not with the isolation of variables or the control of bureaucratic deviations from centrally-designed blueprints, but with effectively engaging the necessary participation of system members in contributing to the collective knowledge of the system.

He contends that "the more complex the problem, the greater the need for localized solutions and for value innovations – both of which call for broadly based participation in decision processes," and he points to a number of small-scale development projects in Asia that have used these processes more successfully than those that were planned and managed by conventional methods. Korten and Carner (1982: 10–12) show that bureaucracies such as the National Irrigation Administration in the Philippines can be organized in ways that allow them to be responsive to the needs of local communities and that allow participation by a wide variety of interest groups and beneficiaries in planning and managing development projects. The Communal Irrigation Committee (CIC) was set up by the NIA to guide pilot irrigation projects, mobilize institutional resources, pull together professionals from various agencies and institutions affecting irrigation programs with local leaders into a coalition for change, and provide direction and guidance for centrally initiated but locally managed development. The CIC does not impose a set of organizational relationships on a community but serves "to legitimize existing relationships and processes." Membership on the committee is voluntary and members join and leave as projects progress and as their interests dictate. The functional benefits of the committee compel some members to remain and provide continuity. The processes of planning and management are based on experience with irrigation projects in different communities rather than being controlled by centrally determined rules and regulations.

But learning-based administration implies the need to go beyond new organizational arrangements to educate and train individuals in the process of joining action with learning. John Friedmann (1973) notes that there are four essential elements of individual learning on which the process must be based: (1) the ability to question existing reality and to raise questions about existing practices, relationships and conditions, not only to understand and cope with them more effectively but also to appreciate how and when to make needed changes; (2) the ability to draw general lessons from particular experience, which in turn requires sharpened observation and inductive reasoning; (3) the ability to test theory in practice so that actions can be infused with and guided by experience; and (4) the ability to examine results in an objective and sincere way in order to uncover and examine mistakes as well as to apply successful approaches in new situations. None of these elements, of course, is easy to apply in conventional bureaucracies, which are organized to standardize, routinize and limit individual discretion. Finding ways of inculcating the spirit of learning, experimentation and creativity in hierarchical bureaucracies remains a challenge for development administrators.

DEVELOPING WIDESPREAD AND APPROPRIATE FORMS OF ADMINISTRATIVE CAPACITY

Governments of developing countries and international assistance agencies have given relatively little attention to alternative ways of organizing for development. International agencies have either left governments to their own devices or insisted on administrative arrangements that conform to Western administrative principles.

Recent experience with development, however, suggests that the ability of planners and managers to implement projects and programs as policy experiments depends on building administrative capacity at all levels in developing societies, both by involving a wider range of organizations and by decentralizing authority and responsibility. Esman and Montgomery (1980) have pointed out that human resource development programs require a variety of organizational arrangements for eliciting the participation of those who are to be affected by the projects, and for assuring that resources reach the intended groups. In addition to using centrally financed and managed bureaucracies, programs should be administered through modified bureaucracies that can be released from conventional central controls to extend their reach in unconventional ways. Local authorities often have linkages of interaction with local groups that central bureaucracies do not know about and cannot reach. Market mechanisms may be used more effectively to deliver services with only modest government intervention. Many voluntary organizations have ties and channels of distribution to groups that are frequently identified as beneficiaries of social and economic development projects, and through which experimental, pilot and demonstration projects can be carried out. Finally, it is necessary to build the administrative capacity of, and involve in planning and administration, what Esman and Montgomery call "organized special publics": interest groups such as credit unions, women's clubs, irrigation associations, labor unions and cooperatives. Thus, constituencies are created that will support projects for their members and act as channels of interaction between beneficiaries and the agencies sponsoring development programs. Once mobilized these organizations can also begin to generate their own projects, thereby supplementing and extending the impact of government sponsored ones.

At the same time, if implementation is to be improved, policy-makers in developing countries must begin to practice what Jon Moris (1977) calls "engaged planning." Moris argues that policies and programs often cannot be implemented successfully by existing bureaucracies through routine administration. Special arrangements must often be made to protect and promote new programs until they are institutionalized. He contends that in East Africa "development does not occur under either private or socialist auspices unless someone regularly puts in a large margin of extra 'intelligence' effort of a managerial nature" (Moris, 1977: 127). Either individuals with a high degree of motivation to achieve program goals must be placed in charge of these activities or special implementation units must be created to administer the programs outside of the regular bureaucratic structure. In any case, Moris (1977: 127) argues that: "Somebody must keep the daily activities of distinct but vertically interlocked services under surveillance, must frame contingency plans, . . . must indulge in bureaucratic politics in order to secure the commitments implied in action programmes, and must be prepared even to break the rules in an emergency."

In developing countries choices among organizational arrangements must consider the trade-off between the costs of apparent redundancy and duplication and the increased probabilities of succeeding in attaining development goals. Some analysts argue that the creation of redundancy, far from being inefficient and wasteful, is essential for increasing the reliability of service delivery. Caiden and Wildavsky (1974) point out that the ability of rich countries to obtain the resources needed for production and service delivery owes less to management efficiency than to complex redundancy. When a large number of organizations with resources and skills are performing the same or similar functions, the failure of one organization is not critical. Others fill the gap, thereby greatly increasing reliability and reducing uncertainty. "Arrangements in poor countries," they note (p. 63), "lack the benefits of redundancy — the surplus, the reserve, the overlapping networks of skills and data — to cushion the reverberating effects of uncertainty."

Some governments and international assistance agencies, such as the World Bank, attempt to avoid the constraints and weaknesses of public administration by creating autonomous implementation units for each large-scale project. These institutions are usually outside of the formal government structure and are given the resources necessary to carry out their tasks. Often they can offer higher salaries, better benefits and amenities, have greater flexibility to innovate and act expeditiously, and are able to attract the most competent staff. But the creation of large numbers of autonomous development authorities can also have some disadvantages. Too often they become powers unto themselves and over time amass enough political influence to pursue their own interests, which are in conflict with national development policies. Some may become so dependent on external financial and technical support that they respond more readily to international assistance agency priorities and technical and professional standards than to the needs of their own clientele. Yet, these problems are far less dangerous in most developing countries than not having widespread administrative capacity, for recent experience suggests that it is difficult to control complex and uncertain projects entirely from the center (Rondinelli, 1981; 1982; Cheema and Rondinelli, 1983).

DECENTRALIZING AUTHORITY FOR DEVELOPMENT PLANNING AND ADMINISTRATION

Much more attention must be given to alternative means of decentralizing authority, responsibility and resources for project planning and management from central government ministries through field administration, the creation of local administrative units, delegation of functions to regional, special purpose or functional authorities, and devolution of functions to local governments. A number of advantages have been attributed to decentralization. First, it can make the implementation of national policy more effective by delegating to local officials greater responsibility for tailoring development projects to local conditions and needs. Decentralization would allow local officials to cut through the enormous amounts of "red tape" and the highly bureaucratic procedures characteristic of planning and administration in developing nations that result in part from the over-concentration of power, authority and resources in the central government. By decentralizing development functions to the field offices of ministries, or to subordinate levels of administration, more public servants can become knowledgeable and sensitive to local problems and needs because they will be working at the level where these are most visible and pressing. Closer contact between local populations and government officials could also allow the latter to obtain better information with which to formulate plans and programs than could be obtained in the national capital. Decentralization might also increase political and administrative support for national development policies at the local level, where the plans of the government are often unknown by the local population or are undermined by local elites, and where support for the central government is often weak. Areal decentralization can promote national unity by giving groups in different sections of the country the ability to participate in planning and decision-making and thus to increase their "stake" in maintaining political stability. Decentralization is also prescribed as a way of increasing the efficiency of central agencies by relieving top management of routine, detailed tasks that could more effectively be performed by field staff or local political leaders who can plan more carefully and support implementation more effectively (Rondinelli, 1981: 1982).

An enduring problem of promoting effective and appropriate forms of decentralization in developing countries is what Rondinelli (1979) has called the "paradox of power." A paradox inherent in administrative reforms is that although strong central political commitment is necessary to initiate them, they cannot be effectively implemented and sustained without diffused political support and widespread participation. But those whose political commitment is necessary to initiate the reforms often consider such a diffusion of participation and power as a serious threat. Development projects that reallocate economic resources, increase income and expand participation in the economy also create new and potentially more powerful interest groups that can make claims on and challenge central authority. Indeed, the creation of countervailing power is often a precondition for sustaining organizational reform.

Although many development projects need central guidance and support, their implementation must be localized to meet unique or special needs, especially in rural areas where resources and institutional capability are lacking or weak. Evaluations of rural development projects suggest that devolution of authority for planning and management has generally made them more effective in reaching and serving intended beneficiaries. In his review of land reform programs in twenty-five countries, Montgomery (1972: 62) concluded that devolution of administrative functions to local, non-career officials "produced significantly better results for peasant welfare than arrangements using professional administrators, whether in a centralized or decentralized administrative system." Nelson's (1973: 267) studies of twenty-four land development projects in nine Latin American countries reinforced Montgomery's conclusions. Nelson found no projects with "dynamic performance" among those undertaken by the national government: all economically viable projects were spontaneous colonizations, private efforts, or publicly supported but privately executed ventures. On the other hand, "practically all recorded failures have been state-directed projects."

The record of devolution is also mixed, but there are some clear examples of success. To the extent that communes were given responsibility for a wide variety of local decisions in China, devolution seems to have created motivation and interest on the part of local leaders. It allowed national programs to be tailored to the needs of villages, and gave rural people more control over selecting and implementing small-scale social service projects. Taiwan and Japan both successfully implemented agrarian development programs through a network of local institutions (Smith, 1974). Land reforms in Asian and Latin American countries seem to have worked better when they were decentralized because devolution allowed easier access to information, better communications among various levels of organization, and increased community solidarity and support (Montgomery, 1972).

But serious obstacles to decentralization exist in most developing countries. Few governments have been willing to establish state, provincial, regional or district governments with sufficient autonomy and resources to carry out their tasks or with sufficient power to co-ordinate the work of different ministries operating within their jurisdictions. In nearly all countries, the tensions and conflicts over control and distribution of political power are an underlying factor. The tensions between the desire to maintain central control and the need to diffuse support and elicit participation are evident in all societies attempting to decentralize administrative authority (Rondinelli, 1981; Cheema and Rondinelli, 1983). China's ambivalence toward decentralization, and the recurring shifts during Mao's regime between delegation of authority and recentralization, illustrated the "paradox of power." Ambivalence resulted from fear of the growing power of provincial leaders during periods of decentralization and from their pursuit of regional self-sufficiency in economic development – sometimes in conflict with national plans and policies. In the 1960s, when decentralization threatened to give provincial leaders the power to challenge national policies, communist party leaders pressured Mao to recentralize because "it became more difficult for the central party leadership to elicit compliance from the provinces." As Parris Chang (1972: 29) points out, "the center [had] increasingly found itself compelled to use negotiations, bargaining, cajoling and manipulation in dealing with province authorities." Central control was re-exerted because "provincial leaders appear to have exercised an effective veto power over policy decisions made in Peking."

BUILDING LOCAL ORGANIZATIONAL CAPACITY AND AN EFFECTIVE INSTITUTIONAL NETWORK FOR SERVICE DELIVERY

Yet creating countervailing power widely in developing societies is essential for promoting a more responsive, flexible and adaptive system of planning and administration that can respond more effectively to complexity and uncertainty. If development administration is to respond more effectively to the needs of those groups who traditionally have been bypassed by economic progress, three tasks must be successfully carried out: first, the hold of clientelist politics must be broken; second, it must be replaced with organizations or coalitions strong enough to represent the interests of the poor when decisions about them are made; and third, an effective institutional structure for delivering services and technology and other resources to the poor must be established.

Breaking the hold of clientelist politics

Little can be done to reorder administrative structure and procedures in areas where people are dependent on wealthy landowners or elites for their livelihood and survival, and where such dependence manifests itself in the patrons' domination of local and national politics through personalism, favoritism, and the manipulation and control of large peasant voting blocs (Powell, 1970; Scott, 1972). In places where rural people depend on patrons to purchase their labor and products, provide shelter, offer credit, loans and aid in emergencies or crises, and assist in paying for marriages and funerals, those government programs that threaten to weaken or destroy the patron–client relationship will receive no sympathy from the elite and little support from peasants. In many rural areas the patron–client relationship provides whatever small amount of security the peasants can expect in an uncertain and precarious life. Development projects will have little impact unless they are accompanied by political change and unless the government can displace the functions performed by patrons by providing demonstrably better, more responsive, more reliable services with little risk for the peasant.

Creating an organizational base of political support and local participation

The difference between more effective and less effective development projects has often been the willingness and ability of government to assist in creating an organizational framework for mobilizing leadership, sharing power and decision-making, and expanding economic participation. Gurley (1974: 389) notes that land reform in China during the late 1950s not only redistributed the productive assets by which the peasantry could economically sustain itself, but also and perhaps more importantly organized rural people to break the hold of the landlord-gentry class:

> The Chinese land reform did not *give* land to the poor peasants. It encouraged them to organize themselves to *take* it, and in the process to crush their former oppressors. This was the prerequisite for later social development in the countryside, for, without it, the old class structure and wealth ownership patterns would have been regenerated by the persistence of old attitudes and of institutions favorable to the rich.

Similarly, in Taiwan and Japan the success of agrarian reform projects depended on first breaking the control of wealthy landowners and then substituting strong local government and a network of farmers' associations, irrigation associations, land reform committees, and cooperatives that allowed participation by rural people and provided a channel of communication and influence. In China and a few other countries, rural development depends heavily on the use of political cadres to mobilize participation. Cadres are carefully chosen young volunteers, often high school or college graduates of peasant stock, who are intensively indoctrinated, and are highly motivated to suffer the deprivations and hardships of working and living in the poorest rural areas for long periods of time (Ledesma, 1976).

Organizing for effective service delivery

The capacity of public organizations to deliver services to the poor is one of the most crucial factors affecting the success of rural development projects. To a large extent, subsistence farmers and landless laborers are poor because they lack access to public and private institutions that have the resources needed to increase their productivity and incomes (Rondinelli and Ruddle, 1977; 1978). In many rural regions essential services do not exist or are provided only in traditional forms. The institutions through which social services are usually delivered are either missing or do not serve the majority of people; indeed, they may severely exploit the poor.

Moreover, institutions in rural areas are rarely linked into a network or "hierarchy" of supporting institutions to allow continuous, reliable and efficient flows of services, or they may have low levels of administrative capacity, and are unable to deal with the complex problems of development. New institutions introduced by government or international agencies are frequently so incompatible with traditional practices, customs and behavior that they not only fail to serve, but may further alienate rural people.

Analysts attribute the failure of past attempts at integrated rural development to the absence of or weak linkages among rural organizations. In the future, Ruttan (1975: 12) argues, strategies must aim at "a unique combination of technical and institutional change." Private markets are inaccessible or exploitive, and the public markets "through which political resources are brought to bear on institutional performance in rural areas are often more imperfect – more biased against rural people – than the credit and product markets." Although the concept of appropriate technology is well established, relatively little attention has been given to its organizational dimensions or, more importantly, to the characteristics of appropriate institutions for delivering social services and technological improvements to rural areas.

Adaptive institutions for integrated rural development have a number of important characteristics (Rondinelli and Ruddle, 1977).

First, like appropriate technology, they must be highly adaptable to the wide variety of problems and conditions found in developing countries. Beneficiaries are often quite heterogeneous; small farmers have different needs than shifting cultivators and landless laborers. Moreover, their settlement patterns are usually so unlike that a delivery system designed to meet the needs of only one group will overlook or inadequately serve the others. Organizational solutions can no more be designed and universally prescribed for all rural areas than they can for all developing countries.

Second, rural institutions must be complementary and integrated. Services and technologies must be mutually reinforcing and interlocking in order to stimulate local development. Credit delivered without technical assistance, improved agricultural methods, higher yielding seed varieties, fertilizers, irrigation and improved marketing have made little impact on production and income in rural areas in most developing countries. Institutions must be linked both vertically and horizontally to provide a hierarchy of services and to increase the quality and reliability of delivery. In their studies of Asian countries, Uphoff and Esman (1974: xi) "found no case where only one institution was carrying the full responsibility for rural development or where *complementarities* among institutions were not as important as what the institutions themselves did."

Third, adaptive organizations must be built on culturally accepted arrangements, practices and behavior. Understanding traditional institutions that have served rural people for decades or centuries, their strengths, inadequacies, limitations and potentials for transformation, is essential for modifying old arrangements and introducing new ones. The success of agrarian reform in Taiwan and Japan was largely attributed to the modification of traditional farmers' associations for new functions in land redistribution and community development. Even after the revolution in China, Mao's planners were careful to adopt acceptable local arrangements as the basis of communal structure. The communal system, as Stavis (1974: 54–5) points out, "did not emerge from an historical and social vacuum; it was not simply proclaimed according to a vision of society." On the contrary, the communes were "intimately related to centuries of economic and political history and to almost a decade of gradually expanding organs of economic cooperation, slowly increasing in size, complexity, responsibility and degree of socialization."

Fourth, as the Chinese experience demonstrates, the institutional network must be designed to transform traditional practices and behavior into more suitable arrangements for economic growth and equitable income distribution. Although they must be based on and compatible with rural custom and tradition, they must also be catalysts for change, transforming developmentally inadequate practices and behavior at a locally acceptable pace. Moreover, they must gradually displace those traditional institutions that are incapable of change and remain flexible enough themselves to be adapted to changing conditions as development occurs.

Fifth, adaptive institutions must tailor service delivery arrangements to the locational requirements of their rural clientele, which in most cases means modifying the "central service point" locational bias of large-scale organizations. Rather than locating organizations that deliver basic services in large cities or provincial capitals, which are not usually accessible to rural residents, they should be located in district capitals or large villages or their services must be brought to rural clients through mobile or widely dispersed delivery mechanisms. Rural people would be sought out at farmsteads, or services would be brought to marketplaces; officials would travel to the rural areas rather than requiring rural people to go to centrally located government offices. Taiwan, Korea and, to some extent, the Philippines have been able to mobilize rural savings and provide financial services by extending banking functions through widely dispersed branch offices, using mobile and temporary facilities in villages on market days, and creating agricultural and fishing financing associations and credit cooperatives in rural areas (Villanueva, 1971; Maithreyan, 1965). The short-term costs of these arrangements undoubtedly are higher than fixed-point service delivery, but they are also more effective in reaching small-scale farmers and rural workers.

Finally, adaptive institutions must be designed in conjunction with beneficiaries and open to local participation and leadership. Efficient and effective service delivery to the rural poor can rarely be attained through standardized locational criteria or by mechanisms designed by professional technicians and administrators. It depends on an intimate understanding of rural life, behavior and motivation, which is unlikely to be brought to bear on the planning and implementation of integrated rural development programs without participation of intended beneficiaries (Ruddle and Rondinelli, 1983).

RELYING ON ADJUNCTIVE AND STRATEGIC RATHER THAN COMPREHENSIVE AND CONTROL-ORIENTED PLANNING

In their now classic study of planning and budgeting procedures in developing nations, Caiden and Wildavsky (1974: 293) concluded that "if we were asked to design a mechanism for decisions to maximize every known disability and minimize any possible advantage of poor countries, we could hardly do better than comprehensive, multi-sectoral planning." Drawing on reviews of planning and budgeting processes in eighty developing countries they confirmed many of the assertions made in chapters 2 and 3 of this study, that comprehensive planning "calls for unavailable information, nonexistent knowledge, and a political stability in consistent pursuit of aims undreamed of in their existence. Thus, this kind of planning turns the most characteristic features of poor countries into obstacles to development."

Improving the administration of complex and uncertain policies requires new forms of planning. Adjunctive and strategic planning must be substituted for comprehensive analysis and central control. Adjunctive planning seeks to facilitate decision-making among a wide variety of organizations and interests in society, focus attention on solving remediable aspects of known problems, identify courses of action that move marginally, incrementally and through successive approximation away from unsatisfactory social and economic conditions even when "optimal" or ideal goals cannot be agreed upon, and explore alternatives on which diverse interests can act jointly (Rondinelli: 1971; 1975).

Strategic planning falls between the extremes of revolution as an instrument of social change and tool-oriented or technological approaches to administration that reinforce the status quo. Undoubtedly there are countries in which significant changes in policy, perspective and procedures cannot be brought about, and in which adaptive administration would be impossible, without revolutionary change. But revolution, because it is an extreme form of change, can be used effectively as an instrument of social policy only under very special and infrequently occurring conditions. Cleaves (1980: 298) points out that revolution is only possible

> at specific moments of social disjunction, and is not often an event that can be planned in detail beforehand. Even when such drastic change occurs and progressive political leadership takes advantage of it, problems emerge concerning how to direct the energies that are unleashed. Attending to the short-term individualistic or material values that motivate many popular sectors may help sweep away the offenders of a pernicious system, but may also result in a new set of relationships that is little more economically or socially advantageous to the poor and, more importantly, has no effect on consolidating their power for future initiatives.

If revolutions fail, they may strengthen the position of entrenched interests and make them less responsive and adaptive in implementing policy. If they succeed, their leaders still face the complex problems of organizing the bureaucracy to carry out uncertain development programs and projects. Revolutions may simply result in one set of elites replacing another, or may so disrupt the social and political order that government becomes incapacitated for a long period of time. The task of transforming bureaucracies and organizing poor groups in societies still remains a long and arduous task. "When revolutionary leadership fails to do so, or abandons the task," Cleaves (1980: 299) points out, "a possibility exists for counter-revolutionary forces to fill the gap." And even in post-revolutionary societies all of the factors that influence policy implementation cannot be anticipated and controlled from the center.

In stable political situations, it is especially important that planning and administration be strategic and adjunctive. Lindblom (1975) describes three underlying principles of strategic analysis and planning.

First, analysis is limited to courses of action that produce incremental changes in existing conditions, moving away from undesirable states toward those on which varying political interests can agree. This makes the tasks of analysis and planning more manageable in complex, uncertain or risky situations. Strategic planning begins with what is known and attempts to broaden the base of knowledge and to formulate alternative interventions that will set other changes in motion, rather than beginning with sweeping and comprehensive reforms, the effectiveness and feasibility of which cannot be predicted.

Second, strategic planning seeks to convert large, complex development problems into smaller, disaggregated ones that can be dealt with incrementally. This reduces the complexity of analysis, allowing better use of information and permitting a reconsideration of goals and means as unanticipated forces appear during project implementation. Breaking-up large development problems into components that can be dealt with through smaller-scale projects has strong advantages. Chambers (1978: 211) has pointed out that "big projects can be a trap." Once initial commitments are made to undertake large, complex projects, forces are often set in motion that make the commitments irreversible and that overwhelm planners and administrators after the projects are underway. Moreover, decisions are more easily constrained and choices foreclosed in large projects than in smaller ones. He notes that "the 'yes–no' decision begins to close and often closes before any formal cost-benefit analysis can be carried out."

Caiden and Wildavsky (1974: 309) had earlier concluded from their analysis of planning and budgeting in poor countries that large projects "encase probable errors in concrete." They argued that breaking down development activities into smaller projects could facilitate strategic planning and "greatly increases the prospects of learning, adaptation and correction." They contend that:

Because less has been invested in each individual project, it is relatively less expensive to end them. Since all are not supposed to survive, there is less concern that each will have to be continued or prove productive. Damage can be contained in size and scope. By investing future resources in similar ventures, the good can be built upon. The multiplicity of efforts, the redundancy if you will, increases likelihood that a variety of approaches to the same problem will be tried and that some will work. Projects thus are used, not to carry out existing knowledge, likely to be lacking, but to obtain knowledge through action. . . . As the size of each project is reduced, the demand for information will decline. There is less need to consider the interaction of this small project with others and less dependence upon market information further away in space and time. Because they can be allowed to fail, present projects may be looked at as hypotheses that can be falsified by unfolding events, thus improving the chance for future projects to stand the test of experience.

Third, strategic and adjunctive planning focus on the examination of goals in close connection with emerging values and with the availability of resources to achieve them. They encourage interaction with the groups that must participate in or benefit from projects. This requires planners to examine alternatives in the light of the values embedded in current behavior and attitudes, cultural traditions and economic and political constraints rather than formulating strategies in the "splendid isolation" of the headquarters of international assistance organization or national planning agencies.

SIMPLIFYING PLANNING AND MANAGEMENT PROCEDURES

It is also clear from past experience that administrative procedures and arrangements for development must be relatively simple and uncomplicated. Their purposes must be clearly defined. Complex managerial methods rarely work at any level of government in developing countries, and especially at the local level in rural areas. Rural people either ignore complex administrative procedures or are exploited by government officials who manipulate them. Moreover, skills and resources for management are in short supply in rural areas of most developing nations and administrative capacity will remain relatively weak. Chambers and Belshaw (1973: 6.8) concluded from their experience with the management of rural development programs in Kenya that "in designing management procedures, the temptation is to introduce more and more requirements and measures, more and more complicated techniques and more and more elaborate relationships. But such an approach quickly leads to a drop in output and eventually to paralysis."

The tendency of management scientists to insist on sophisticated and complicated methods of analysis, planning and programming often creates more problems than it solves. Reporting on the results of a symposium on methods of cost-benefit analysis in the appraisal and selection of development projects, Galal Amin (1978: 230) noted that there is a tendency for economists to equate complexity with sophistication. But, "true sophistication might lie in seeing ways in which one could simplify, or short-circuit a long route by adopting a much shorter and simpler plan." Often there is a need for more common sense rather than more rigorous analyses. Defining common sense as the "store of information which men collect through their various experiences but which is very difficult to spell out, let alone quantify," Amin (1978: 232) maintains that it is captured in the judgment or intuition of experienced administrators and leaders.

Less complicated techniques of planning and analysis can provide greater opportunities for experienced planners and administrators to bring their experience to bear on the selection of appropriate projects. Chambers (1978) suggests displacing sophisticated techniques of cost-benefit appraisal with simple decision matrices, ranking systems that focus on the effects of alternative projects on intended beneficiaries, checklists of desired project characteristics, and approximate cost comparisons rather than elaborate rate-of-return and cost-benefit studies. In view of the high degree of uncertainty and the paucity and un-reliability of data in most developing countries, such simplified methods of analysis may be not only quite adequate but also more optimal and cost-effective than complex and "sophisticated" methods. Analytical techniques might then be perceived of as aids to judgment rather than as substitutes for it.

Care must also be taken to keep the design of development projects, especially those intended for rural areas, from becoming too complex. In his extensive review of integrated rural development projects, Cohen (1979: 66) points out that the "more complex an integrated rural development project, the less likely donor agencies or national govern-ments will encourage local participation in the design or implementation of the project, tending to confine participation to sharing in project benefits." He also notes that the experience with such projects shows that the more complex they become, the more difficult it is to obtain cooperation from and maintain coordination among the many organiz-ations and groups that are needed to provide services and inputs. Unless the project has unusually strong political support from the national government, or is organized as an independent implementation unit, it is unlikely that coordinative arrangements can be created or effectively sustained.

ENCOURAGING ERROR DETECTION AND CORRECTION RATHER THAN SUPPRESSION AND PUNISHMENT

One of the most difficult changes to make in the bureaucracies of both international development agencies and developing country govern-ments will be the administrators' attitudes toward error. Under conditions of uncertainty, errors and mistakes are not only likely, they are to be expected. The concept of development policy-making as social experimentation requires that projects be designed in such a way that errors and mistakes can be uncovered as a project proceeds. It can then be redesigned and revised incrementally. Yet the bureaucratic systems in most developing countries, as well as in some international agencies, are designed to suppress mistakes and errors and to punish managers when mistakes are discovered. Such attitudes are not only unrealistic but also dangerous. They cause administrators and managers to be fearful of making mistakes, encourage them to cover up or deny the existence of errors, and to discourage correction, redesign and redirection. They inhibit creativity, innovation, flexibility and experimentation – the very stuff of successful project management. Moreover, they prevent planners and administrators from involving other groups and organizations in decision-making, thereby obstructing the process of gathering the information and tapping the experience needed to make projects more relevant and successful. Because of their fear of error detection, managers avoid evaluation and monitoring, instead of using these procedures as essential tools of learning.

Learning by doing can become acceptable only when it is explicitly recognized that all development projects are basically social experiments. Incentives and rewards must be provided to encourage innovation, experimentation and creativity. Only uncorrected errors should be considered evidence of poor management. The ability of managers and administrators to monitor and evaluate continuously, so that mistakes are uncovered and corrected quickly, must be strengthened in the bureaucracies of developing countries and international assistance organizations.

CREATING INCENTIVES FOR INNOVATIVE MANAGEMENT

Administrative systems and procedures are needed that encourage, support and reward those managers who take responsibility for development activities – especially in rural areas where uncertainty and risk of failure are greater and where the knowledge required to plan and implement projects comprehensively and systematically is least likely to be available. The unwillingness of public administrators in most developing countries to work outside of the national capital and in local and provincial governments is not only due to a civil service system that is structured to reward service in central ministries and agencies, but also because civil servants perceive that their specialized skills would not be appreciated or rewarded in the provinces. The attempts to decentralize development planning and administration in the Sudan during the

1970s, for example, were strongly opposed by technicians and professionals in the central ministries who feared that in the provinces they would not get adequate support from local officials (Rondinelli, 1982). The reluctance of central government officials to serve in rural areas is also attributable to the substantial differences in living conditions between the national capital and smaller cities and towns. Living conditions for professionals in the Sudan tend to be far lower in the provinces, where housing is inadequate, educational opportunities for children are limited, supplies and equipment are difficult to obtain from the capital, and there are few opportunities for professional advancement. The inability or unwillingness of national governments to provide suitable living conditions and incentives for civil servants to work in the provinces threatens the success of decentralized development projects and severely weakens the capacity of the central government to provide needed technical and managerial support to local administration.

After reviewing a variety of urban and rural development programs in Zambia, Peru, India, Colombia, Mexico, Kenya and Brazil, Cleaves (1980: 296) concluded that an essential element in improving administration in developing countries is that "national leaders and policy makers must change their frame of reference as to the *definition of personal and policy success* and reward policy implementors accordingly." He argues that administrators who are assigned to risky projects or remote areas must be specially and visibly rewarded when they carry out their tasks successfully:

> When money is limited, quality personnel in outlying districts scarce, and possibilities for change marginal, administrators who undertake these assignments must be recompensed, in terms of remuneration and prestige, for handling small budgets, working in difficult terrains, and accomplishing small, gradual and continuous change. The policy must contain self-evident measures of social improvement so that administrators can record their progress. While appeals for altruism are legitimate ways to build motivation, they cannot completely substitute for direct compensation, especially when implementors sense that they are bearing the brunt of responsibility for national development.

An essential part of the incentive system must be adequate training, a strong system of field support and greater recognition of the special conditions under which field staff work. Esman and Montgomery (1980) have found that the field staff who work with the poor and those populations living in remote areas are usually the worst trained, the least supervised and weakest motivated, and that they are rarely supported by efficient supply systems. The capacity of field administrators to work with beneficiary groups must be strengthened and their ability to mobilize human and financial resources in ways that foster mutual respect and cooperation between government administrators and local residents must be improved. In many countries this means finding ways of changing the attitudes and behavior of government officials toward the public and toward the purposes of their jobs. The work of administrators should be facilitating and supporting rather than control-oriented. Field administrators must be trained to recognize the capacity of local residents, regardless of their social status, level of education or income, to make important contributions of knowledge, skills or commitment to the success of development activities.

Moreover, after field administrators and project managers are trained, they must be given discretion to manage without the rigid supervision that smothers flexibility and creativity. If they are to be effective they must be given adequate resources to obtain the equipment, supplies, personnel and facilities needed to carry out their tasks. Upward mobility within the civil service system must be tied to field performance. As long as field service posts are perceived of as inferior, unrewarded and dead-end positions, ambitious and skilled managers will resist field assignments and continue to seek positions at headquarters in the national capital.

CONCLUSIONS

Equitable development requires expanding administrative capacity throughout developing societies. It implies expanding participation in economic activities, drawing larger numbers of people into processes of production, exchange and consumption, mobilizing savings and investing them in directly productive and social services and facilities. It means expanding the capacity of a wide variety of public and private organizations to plan and carry out decisions affecting them and increasing the access of individuals to resources and opportunities needed to meet their basic human needs, raise their productivity and develop human potential. Courses of action that lead to the attainment of these objectives will remain complex and uncertain. Solving societal problems will depend on the ability of planners and administrators to use more effectively the political, social and economic mechanisms of authority, exchange and persuasion, which Lindblom (1977) argues are the fundamental means of promoting social change.

Development planners and administrators must not only understand these mechanisms better but also learn how to combine them in new ways to cope with complexity and uncertainty. Lindblom's (1977: 6) observation of India applies as well to many other developing countries: "India's difficulties in economic development are in part the consequences of her leaders' inability to understand that growth requires a growth mechanism; if not the market, which Indian policy cripples, then the authority of government, which India has never chosen to mobilize."

In either case, effective development administration is unlikely to emerge from conventional principles, which emphasize comprehensive, detailed and control-oriented planning and management. In an uncertain and complex world, planning and administration must be adaptive. They require managers who can facilitate rather than control the interaction of those individuals and groups who have the bits of knowledge, resources and experience needed to change undesirable conditions and the judgment to help define what the undesirable conditions are. Adaptive administration requires skilled people who can act as catalysts, mobilizing those whose support or commitment is needed to make development programs and projects responsive, appropriate and successful. It demands administrators who can respond creatively and quickly to changes, who are willing and able to seek out and correct mistakes as they are discovered, and who can plan and manage simultaneously. It requires administrators who view themselves as leaders rather than as bureaucrats. It calls for managerial systems in international organizations and governments of developing countries that train administrators to join action with learning, to experiment, to test new ways of doing things and to be sensitive and responsive to the needs of the people they serve. Most of all, it requires administrative systems that let good managers manage, and that reward them for their efforts and results. Finding new ways of establishing conditions that allow development administrators to recognize and cope effectively with the inevitable complexity and uncertainty of development problems will be the strongest challenge to developing countries and international assistance agencies in the remaining years of this century.

NOTE

1 This chapter is an expanded version of an article by the author, "The Dilemma of Development Administration: Uncertainty and Complexity in Control-Oriented Bureaucracies," which appeared in *World Politics*, vol. XXXV, no. 1 (October 1982). It also draws heavily on the author's article, "Administration of Integrated Rural Development: The Politics of Agrarian Reform in Developing Countries," *World Politics*, vol. XXXI, no. 3 (April 1979). Material from both is reprinted here with the permission of Princeton University Press.

Bibliography

Adelman, I. (1975) "Growth, Income Distribution and Equity-Oriented Development Strategies," *World Development*, 2–3 (3), 67–76.

Adelman, I. and C. Morris (1967) *Society, Politics and Economic Development*, Baltimore, Md, Johns Hopkins University Press.

Adelman, I. and C. Morris (1973) *Economic Growth and Social Equity in Developing Countries*, Stanford, Calif., Stanford University Press.

Ahmad, Y. (1977) "Project Identification, Analysis and Preparation in Developing Countries: A Discursive Commentary," in D. Rondinelli (ed.) *Planning Development Projects*, Stroudsburg, Pa, Hutchinson & Ross, 161–5.

Amin, G. (1978) "Themes from the Discussion at the Symposium," *World Development*, 2 (6), 227–40.

APHA (1977) *The State of the Art of Developing Low Cost Health Services in Developing Countries*, Washington, D.C., American Public Health Association.

Bainbridge, J. and S. Sapire (1974) *Health Project Management*, Geneva, World Health Organization.

Baum, W. (1978) "The World Bank Project Cycle," *Finance and Development*, 4 (15), 10–17.

Benveniste, G. (1972) *The Politics of Expertise*, Berkeley, Calif., Glendessary Press.

Braybrooke, D. and C. Lindblom (1970) *A Strategy of Decision*, New York, Free Press.

Bromley, R. (1981) "From Cavalry to White Elephant: A Colombian Case of Urban Renewal and Marketing Reform," *Development and Change* (12), 77–120.

Bromley, R. and E. Bustelo (1982) "Introduction," in Bromley and Bustelo (eds) *Politica x Technica No Planajamento: Perspectivas Criticas*, Brasilia, UNICEF, 9–11.

Brown, D. (1971) *Agricultural Development in India's Districts*, Cambridge, Mass., Harvard University Press.

Burki, S. (1980) "Sectoral Priorities for Meeting Basic Needs," *Finance and Development*, 1 (17), 18–22.

Burns, T. and G. Stalker (1961) *The Management of Innovation*, London, Tavistock.

Caiden, N. and A. Wildavsky (1974) *Planning and Budgeting in Poor Countries*, New York, Wiley.

Ceylon, Government of (1959) *The Ten Year Plan for Ceylon*, Colombo, Government Press.

Chambers, R. (1978) "Project Selection for Poverty Focused Rural Development: Simple is Optimal," *World Development* (6), 209–19.

Chambers, R. and D. Belshaw (1973) *Managing Rural Development: Lessons and Methods from East Africa*, Brighton, Institute of Development Studies, University of Sussex.

Chang, P. (1972) "Centralization versus Decentralization in the Chinese Political System, 1949–1971," *Asian Forum*, 3 (4), 14–36.

Changrien, P. (1970) *Development Planning in Thailand*, unpublished Ph.D. dissertation, Ann Arbor, Mich., University Microfilms.

Cheema, G. S. and D. Rondinelli (1983) "Introduction," in Cheema and Rondinelli (eds) *Decentralization and Development: Policy Implementation in Developing Countries*, Beverly Hills, Calif., Sage Publications.

Chenery, H. (1974) "Introduction," in H. Chenery *et al. Redistribution with Growth*, London, Oxford University Press, xiii–xx.

Choldin, H. (1969) "The Development Project as a Natural Experiment: The Comilla, Pakistan Project," *Economic Development and Cultural Change* (17), 483–500.

Cleaves, P. (1980), "Implementation Amidst Scarcity and Apathy: Political Power and Policy Design," in M. Grindle (ed.) *Politics and Policy Implementation in The Third World*, Princeton, N.J., Princeton University Press, 281–303.

Cohen, J. (1974) "Rural Change in Ethiopia: The Chilalo Agricultural Development Unit," *Economic Development and Cultural Change* (22), 580–614.

Cohen, J. (1979) *Integrating Services for Rural Development*, Discussion Paper, Cambridge, Mass., Harvard Institute for International Development.

Cole, D. and P. Lyman (1971) *Korean Development: The Interplay of Politics and Economics*, Cambridge, Mass., Harvard University Press.

Crane, B. and J. Finkle (1981) "Organizational Impediments to Development Assistance: The World Bank's Population Program," *World Politics* 4 (33), 516–33.

Cuca, R. and C. Pierce (1977) *Experiments in Family Planning: Lessons from the Developing World*, Baltimore, Md, Johns Hopkins University Press.

Currie, L. (1966) *Accelerating Development*, New York, McGraw-Hill.

Das, N. (1973) "India's Planning Experience," *World Today* (October), 430–9.

Davis, J. (1974) *An Introduction to Public Administration*, New York, Free Press.

Esman, M. (1969) "Institution Building as a Guide to Action," unpublished paper, Washington, D.C., US Agency for International Development.

Esman, M. (1972) *Administration of Development in Malaysia*, Ithaca, N.Y., Cornell University Press.

Esman, M. (1977) "Monitoring the Progress of Projects: The Redbook and Operations Room in Malaysia," in D. Rondinelli (ed.) *Planning Development Projects*, Stroudsburg, Pa, Hutchinson & Ross, 225–9.

Esman, M. and J. Montgomery (1980) "The Administration of Human Development," in P. Knight (ed.) *Implementing Programs of Human Development*, World Bank Staff Working Paper No. 403, Washington, D.C., World Bank, 183–234.

Ewing, A. (1974) "Pre-Investment," *Journal of World Trade Law* (8), 316–28.

Frankel, F. (1971) *India's Green Revolution*, Princeton, N.J., Princeton University Press.

Friedman, M. (1958) "Foreign Economic Aid: Means and Objectives," in G. Ranis (ed.) *The United States and the Developing Economies*, New York, Norton, 250–63.

Friedmann, J. (1973) *Retracking America: A Theory of Transactive Planning*, Garden City, New York, Anchor Press.

Gittinger, J. (1972) *Economic Analysis of Agricultural Projects*, Baltimore, Md, Johns Hopkins University Press.

Gordenker, L. (1976) *International Aid and National Decisions: Development Programs in Malawi, Tanzania and Zambia*, Princeton, N.J., Princeton University Press.

Grant, J. (1973) "Development: The End of Trickle Down?" *Foreign Policy* (12), 42–65.

Griffin, K. B. and J. Enos (1970) "Foreign Assistance: Objectives and Consequences," *Economic Development and Cultural Change* (118), 313–27.

Griffin, K. and A. Khan (1978) "Poverty in the Third World: Ugly Facts and Fancy Models," *World Development*, 3 (6), 295–304.

Grindle, M. (1977) *Bureaucrats, Politicians and Peasants in Mexico*, Berkeley, University of California Press.

Gurley, J. (1974) "Rural Development in China," in E. Edwards (ed.) *Employment in Developing Nations*, New York, Columbia University Press, 383–403.

Hapgood, D. (1965) *Policies for Promoting Agricultural Development*, Cambridge, Mass., MIT Center for International Studies.

Haque, W., N. Mehta, A. Rahman and P. Wignaraja (1977) "Micro Level Development: Design and Evaluation of Rural Development Projects," *Development Dialogue* (2), 71–137.

Harbison, F. (1962) "Human Resources Development Planning in Modernizing Economies," *International Labour Review*, 5 (85), 2–23.

Heginbotham, S. (1975) *Cultures in Conflict: The Four Faces of Indian Bureaucracy*, New York, Columbia University Press.

Henderson, P. D. (1980) "What's Wrong with the Brandt Report?: Economics Askew," *Encounter* (December), 12–17.

Hirschman, A. (1959) *The Strategy of Economic Development*, New Haven, Conn., Yale University Press.

Hirschman, A. (1967) *Development Projects Observed*, Washington D.C., Brookings Institution.

Hoos, I. (1972) *Systems Analysis in Public Policy: A Critique*, Berkeley, University of California Press.

Hoselitz, B. (1964) "Advanced and Underdeveloped Countries: A Study in Development Contrasts," in W. Hamilton (ed.) *The Transfer of Institutions*, Durham, N.C., Duke University Press, 27–58.

Humphrey, D. (1962) "Indonesia's National Plan for Economic Development," *Asian Survey*, 10 (2), 12–21.

Hussain, I. (1973) "Mechanics of Development Planning in Pakistan: A Suggested Framework," *Pakistan Economic and Social Review*, 4 (2), 454–62.

Hutchinson, E., C. Montrie, J. Hawes and F. Mann (1974) *Intercountry Evaluation of Agricultural Sector Programs*, vol. 4, Washington, D.C., US Agency for International Development.

Ickis, J. (1981) "Structural Responses to New Rural Development Strategies," in D. Korten and F. Alfonso (eds) *Bureaucracy and the Poor: Closing the Gap*, Singapore, McGraw-Hill, 4–32.

Independent Commission on International Development (Brandt Report) (1980) *North–South: A Program for Survival*, Cambridge, Mass., MIT Press.

Institute of Development Studies (IDS) (1972) *An Overall Evaluation of the Special Rural Development Program*, Occasional Paper No. 8, Nairobi, University of Nairobi.

International Labor Office (1976) *Tripartite World Conference on Employment, Income Distribution and Social Progress and the International*

Division of Labor, Declaration of Principles and Program of Action, Geneva, ILO.

Jackson, R. (1969) *A Study of the Capacity of the United Nations System*, Geneva, United Nations.

Johnston, B. and W. Clark (1982) *Redesigning Rural Development: A Strategic Perspective*, Baltimore, Md, Johns Hopkins University Press.

Johnston, B. and J. Mellor (1961) "The Role of Agriculture in Economic Development," *American Economic Review*, 4 (51), 571–81.

Karunatilake, H. (1971) *Economic Development in Ceylon*, New York, Praeger.

Katz, S. (1970) "Exploring a Systems Approach to Development Administration," in F. Riggs (ed.) *Frontiers of Development Administration*, Durham, N.C., Duke University Press, 109–38.

Khan, A. (1978) "Pakistan – The Daudzai Experiment," in Asian Productivity Organization, *Rural Development Strategies of Selected Member Countries*, Tokyo, APO, 139–45.

Kilby, P. (1979) "Evaluating Technical Assistance," *World Development* (7), 309–23.

Kim, J. K. (1978) "Republic of Korea," in Asian Productivity Organization, *Rural Development Strategies of Selected Member Countries*, Tokyo, APO, 12–20.

Kim, K. and O. Kim (1977) "Korea's Saemaul Undong: Social Structure and the Role of Government in Integrated Rural Development," *Bulletin of Population and Development Studies Center* (6), 1–15.

Korea, Republic of (1971) *The Third Five Year Economic Development Plan 1972–1976*, Seoul, Government Printer.

Korea, Republic of (1980) *Saemaul Undong 1980*, Seoul, Ministry of Home Affairs.

Korten, D. (1980) "Community Organization and Rural Development: A Learning Process Approach," *Public Administration Review*, 5 (40), 480–511.

Korten, D. (1981) "Management of Social Transformation at National and Subnational Levels," unpublished paper, Manila, Ford Foundation.

Korten, D. and F. Alfonso (eds) (1981) *Bureaucracy and the Poor: Closing the Gap*, Singapore, McGraw-Hill.

Korten, D. and G. Carner (1982) "Reorienting Bureaucracies to Serve People: Two Experiences from the Philippines," unpublished paper, Manila, Ford Foundation.

Kulp, E. (1977) *Designing and Managing Basic Agricultural Programs*, Bloomington, Indiana University International Development Institute.

Kuznets, S. (1966) *Modern Economic Growth*, New Haven, Conn., Yale University Press.

Lamb, G. (1982) "Market-Surrogate Approaches to Institutional Development," unpublished paper summarizing the work done by Lamb, A. Israel and B. Shaffer, Washington, D.C., World Bank.

Landau, M. (1970) "Development Administration and Decision Theory," in E. Weidner (ed.) *Development Administration in Asia*, Durham, N.C., Duke University Press, 73–103.

LaPorte, R. Jr. (1970) "Administrative, Political and Social Constraints on Economic Development in Ceylon," *International Review of Administrative Sciences* (35), 158–71.

Ledesma, A. (1976) *Land Reform Programs in East and Southeast Asia: A Comparative Approach*, Research Paper No. 69, Madison, University of Wisconsin Land Tenure Center.

Lee, E. (1977) "Development and Income Distribution: A Case Study of Sri Lanka and Malaysia," *World Development*, 4 (5), 279–89.

Lee, H. B. (1970), "The Role of the Higher Civil Service Under Rapid Social and Economic Change," in E. Weidner (ed.) *Development Administration in Asia*, Durham, N.C., Duke University Press, 107–31.

Lee, H. I. (1969) "Project Selection and Evaluation," in I. Adelman (ed.) *Practical Approaches to Development Planning*, Baltimore, Md, Johns Hopkins University Press, 241–52.

Lele, U. (1975) *The Design of Rural Development: Lessons from Africa*, Baltimore, Md, Johns Hopkins University Press.

Leonard, D. (1977) *Reaching the Peasant Farmer*, Chicago, Ill., University of Chicago Press.

Lewis, A. (1954) "Economic Development with Limited Supplies of Labor," reprinted in A. Agarwala and S. Singh (eds) *The Economics of Underdevelopment*, New York, Oxford University Press, 1970, 440–9.

Lewis, A. (1955) *The Theory of Economic Growth*, London, Allen & Unwin.

Lim, D. (1973) "Malaysia," in Y. Hoong (ed.) *Development Planning in Southeast Asia*, Singapore, Regional Institute for Higher Education and Development.

Lindblom, C. (1965) *The Intelligence of Democracy: Decision-Making Through Mutual Adjustment*, New York, Free Press.

Lindblom, C. (1975) "The Sociology of Planning: Thought and Social Interaction," in M. Bornstein (ed.) *Economic Planning East and West*, Cambridge, Mass., Ballinger Publishing Company, 23–60.

Lindblom, C. (1977) *Politics and Markets*, New York, Basic Books.

McNamara, R. (1973) *Address to the Board of Governors*, Nairobi, World Bank Group.

Maithreyan, B. (1965) "Savings in a Developing Economy – Certain Suggestions for Reform and National Coordination," *Economic Bulletin for Asia and the Pacific* 1 (26), 188–201.

Majone, G. and A. Wildavsky (1978) "Implementation as Evolution", in H. Freeman (ed.) *Policy Studies Review Annual*, vol. 2, Beverly Hills, Calif., Sage Publications, 103–17.

Mangahas, M. and C. Subido (1976) "Development Planning, Appraisal and Performance Evaluation with Special Reference to the Philippines," *Economic Bulletin for Asia and the Pacific*, 1 (27), 13–27.

Marzouk, G. (1972) *Economic Development and Policies: Case Study of Thailand*, Rotterdam, Rotterdam University Press.

Mason, E. and R. Asher (1973) *The World Bank Since Bretton Woods*, Washington, D.C., Brookings Institution.

Meltsner, A. (1976) *Policy Analysts in the Bureaucracy*, Berkeley, University of California Press.

Mikesell, R. (1968) *The Economics of Foreign Aid*, Chicago, Ill., Aldine.

Montgomery, J. (1972) "Allocation of Authority in Land Reform Programs: A Comparative Study of Administrative Processes and Outputs," *Administrative Science Quarterly* (17), 62–75.

Morawetz, D. (1977) *Twenty Five Years of Economic Development, 1950–1975*, Washington, D.C., World Bank.

Moris, J. (1977) "The Transferability of Western Management Concepts and Programs: An East African Perspective," in L. Stifel, J. Coleman and J. Black (eds) *Education and Training for Public Sector Management in Developing Countries*, New York, Rockefeller Foundation, 73–83.

Moris, J. (1981) *Managing Induced Rural Development*, Bloomington, Indiana University International Development Institute.

Morss, E. *et al.* (1975) *Strategies for Small Farmer Development*, Washington, D.C., Development Alternatives Inc.

Mueller, P. and K. Zevering (1969) "Employment Promotion through Rural Development: A Pilot Project in Western Nigeria," *International Labour Review*, 2 (100), 111–30.

Murphy, D., B. Baker and D. Fisher (1974) *Determinants of Project Success*, Chestnut Hill, Mass., Boston College Institute of Management.

Myrdal, G. (1957) *Rich Lands and Poor: The Road to World Prosperity*, New York, Harper & Row.

Myrdal, G. (1970) *An Approach to the Asian Drama*, New York, Vintage Books.

Nelson, M. (1973) *The Development of Tropical Lands: Policy Issues in Latin America*, Baltimore, Md, Johns Hopkins University Press.

Niehoff, R. (1977) "Some Key Operational Generalizations and Issues in the Use of Nonformal Education," in R. Niehoff (ed.) *Nonformal Education and the Rural Poor*, East Lansing, Michigan State University College of Education.

Nigam, S. (1975) *Employment and Income Distribution Approach in Development Plans of African Countries*, Addis Ababa, International Labour Office.

Nophaket, S. (1973) *The Administrative Requirements of Development Planning in Thailand*, unpublished Ph.D. dissertation, Ann Arbor, Mich., University Microfilms.

Noranitipadungkarn, C. (1977) *Bangkok Metropolitan Immediate Water Improvement Program*, Honolulu, Hawaii, East–West Center.

Nurkse, R. (1953) *Problems of Capital Formation in Underdeveloped Countries*, London, Oxford University Press.

Onunkwo, E. (1973) *Sensitivity Analysis in Evaluation of Agricultural Projects in Nigeria*, unpublished Ph.D. dissertation, Ann Arbor, Mich., University Microfilms.

Ostrander, F. (1974) "Botswana Nickel-Copper: A Case Study in Private Investment's Contribution to Economic Development," in J. Barrat (ed.) *Accelerated Development in Southern Africa*, New York, St Martin's Press, 534–49.

Paine, S. (1976) "Balanced Development: Maoist Conception and Chinese Practice," *World Development*, 4 (4), 277–304.

Paolillo, C. (1976) *A Basic Needs Strategy of Development: Staff Report on World Employment Conference*, Washington, D.C., US Government Printing Office.

Pearson, L. (1969) *Partners in Development*, New York, Praeger.

Poats, R. (1972) *Technology for Developing Nations: New Directions for U.S. Technical Assistance*, Washington, D.C., Brookings Institution.

Powell, J. (1970) "Peasant Society and Clientelist Politics," *American Political Science Review*, 2 (44), 411–25.

Prybyla, J. (1979) "Changes in the Chinese Economy: An Interpretation," *Asian Survey*, 5 (19), 409–35.

Pye, L. (1965) "The Concept of Political Development," *Annals of the Academy of Political and Social Science*, 358, 1–13.

Pyle, D. (1980) "From Pilot Project to Operational Program in India: The Problems of Transition," in M. Grindle (ed.) *Politics and Policy Implementation in the Third World*, Princeton, N.J., Princeton University Press, 123–44.

Quick, S. (1980) "The Paradox of Popularity: Ideological Program Implementation in Zambia," in M. Grindle (ed.) *Politics and Policy Implementation in the Third World*, Princeton, N.J., Princeton University Press, 40–63.

Rahim, S. (1977) "Nonformal Aspects of Comilla Project," in R. Niehoff (ed.) *Nonformal Education and the Rural Poor*, East Lansing, Michigan State University College of Education, 54–68.

Rana, P. (1974) "The Nepalese Economy: Problems and Prospects," *Asian Survey*, 7 (14), 651–62.

Riggs, F. (1970) "Introduction," in F. Riggs (ed.) *Frontiers of Development Administration*, Durham, N.C., Duke University Press, 3–37.

Rondinelli, D. (1971) "Adjunctive Planning and Urban Development Policy," *Urban Affairs Quarterly*, 1 (7), 13–39.

Rondinelli, D. (1975) *Urban and Regional Development Planning: Policy and Administration*, Ithaca, N.Y., Cornell University Press.

Rondinelli, D. (1976) "Public Planning and Political Strategy," *Long Range Planning*, 2 (9), 75–82.

Rondinelli, D. (1976a) "International Requirements for Project Preparation: Aids or Obstacles to Development Planning?" *Journal of the American Institute of Planners*, 3 (43), 314–26.

Rondinelli, D. (1977) "Planning and Implementing Development Projects: An Introduction," in D. Rondinelli (ed.) *Planning Development Projects*, Stroudsburg, Pa, Hutchinson & Ross.

Rondinelli, D. (1978) "National Investment Planning and Equity Policy in Developing Countries: The Challenge of Decentralized Administration," *Policy Sciences*, 1 (10), 45–74.

Rondinelli, D. (1979) "Administration of Integrated Rural Development: The Politics of Agrarian Reform in Developing Countries," *World Politics*, 3 (31), 389–416.

Rondinelli, D. (1979a) "Designing International Development Projects for Implementation," in G. Honadle and R. Klauss (eds) *International Development Administration*, New York, Praeger, 21–52.

Rondinelli, D. (1979b) "Planning Development Projects: Lessons from Developing Countries," *Long Range Planning*, 3 (12), 48–56.

Rondinelli, D. (1981) "Government Decentralization in Comparative Perspective: Theory and Practice in Developing Countries," *International Review of Administrative Sciences*, 2 (47), 133–45.

Rondinelli, D. (1981a) "Administrative Decentralization and Economic Development: Sudan's Experiment with Devolution," *Journal of Modern African Studies*, 4 (19), 595–624.

Rondinelli, D. (1982) "The Dilemma of Development Administration: Uncertainty and Complexity in Control Oriented Bureaucracies," *World Politics*, 1 (35), 43–72.

Rondinelli, D. (1983) "Implementing Decentralization Programs in Asia: A Comparative Analysis," *Public Administration and Development*, 2 (3).

Rondinelli, D. and K. Ruddle (1977) "Local Organization for Integrated Rural Development: Implementing Equity Policy in Developing Countries," *International Review of Administrative Sciences*, 1 (63), 20–30.

Rondinelli, D. and K. Ruddle (1978) *Urbanization and Rural Development: A Spatial Policy for Equitable Growth*, New York, Praeger.

Rosenstein-Rodan, P. (1943) "Problems of Industrialization of Eastern and South Eastern Europe," reprinted in A. Agarwala and S. Singh (eds) *The Economics of Underdevelopment*, New York, Oxford University Press, 1970, 245–55.

Rostow, W. (1952) *The Process of Economic Growth*, New York, Norton.

Ruddle, K. and D. Rondinelli (1983) *Transforming Natural Resources for Human Development*, Tokyo, United Nations University.

Rudner, M. (1975) *Nationalism, Planning and Economic Modernization in Malaysia*, Beverly Hills, Calif., Sage Publications.

Ruttan, V. (1975) "Integrated Rural Development Programs: A Skeptical Perspective," *International Development Review*, 4 (18), 9–16.

Sapolski, H. (1972) *The Polaris Missile System*, Cambridge, Mass., Harvard University Press.

Schick, A. (1973) "A Death in the Bureaucracy: The Demise of Federal PPB," *Public Administration Review*, 2 (33), 146–56.

Schlesinger, J. (1968) "Systems Analysis and the Political Process," *Journal of Law and Economics* (11), 281–98.

Schultz, T. (1964) *Transforming Traditional Agriculture*, New Haven, Conn., Yale University Press.

Schulz, L. (1972) *Politics and Development Planning in Indonesia*, unpublished Ph.D. dissertation, Ann Arbor, Mich., University Microfilms.

Scott, J. (1972) "Patron–Client Politics and Political Change in Southeast Asia," *American Political Science Review*, 1 (46), 91–113.

Seers, D. (1965) "The Limits of the Special Case," *Bulletin of the Oxford Institute of Economics and Statistics*, 2 (25), 77–98.

Self, P. (1975) *Econocrats and the Policy Process: The Politics and Philosophy of Cost-Benefit Analysis*, Boulder, Colo., Westview Press.

Shaefer-Kehnert, W. (1977) "Approaches to the Design of Agricultural Projects," Bloomington, Indiana University International Development Institute.

Siffin, W. (1977) "Two Decades of Public Administration in Developing Countries," in L. Stifle, J. Coleman and J. Black (eds) *Education and Training for Public Sector Management in Developing Countries*, New York, Rockefeller Foundation, 49–60.

Smith, T. (1974) *East Asian Agrarian Reform: Japan, Republic of Korea, Taiwan and the Philippines*, Hartford, Conn., John C. Lincoln Institute.

Spengler, J. (1963) "Bureaucracy and Economic Development," in J. LaPalombara (ed.) *Bureaucracy and Political Development*, Princeton, N.J., Princeton University Press, 199–232.

Stavis, B. (1974) *Peoples Communes and Rural Development in China*, Special Series on Rural Local Government, No. 2, Ithaca, N.Y., Cornell University Center for International Studies.

Strachan, H. (1978) "Side Effects of Planning in the Aid Control System," *World Development*, 4 (6), 467–78.

Streeten, P. (1972) *Frontiers of Development Studies*, New York, Halstead.

Streeten, P. and S. Burki (1978) "Basic Needs: Some Issues," *World Development*, 3 (6), 411–21.

Sussman, G. (1980) "The Pilot Project and the Choice of an Implementing Strategy: Community Development in India," in M. Grindle (ed.) *Politics and Policy Implementation in the Third World*, Princeton, N.J., Princeton University Press, 103–22.

Taylor, K. (1970) "The Pre-Investment Function in the International Development System," *International Development Review*, 2 (12), 2–10.

Tendler, J. (1976) "International Evaluations of Small Farmer Organizations: Ecuador and Honduras," Washington, D.C., US Agency for International Development.

Thimm, H. (1979) *Development Projects in the Sudan*, Tokyo, United Nations University.

Thomas, J. (1974) "Development Institutions, Projects and Aid: A Case Study of the Water Development Program in East Pakistan," *Pakistan Economic and Social Review* (12), 87–103.

Thomas, T. and D. Brinkerhoff (1978) "Devolutionary Strategies for Development Administration," *SICA Occasional Papers*, No. 8, Washington, D.C., American Society for Public Administration, Section on International and Comparative Administration.

Thompson, V. (1964) "Administrative Objectives for Development Administration," *Administrative Science Quarterly* (9), 91–108.

Trapman, C. (1974) *Change in Administrative Structures: A Case Study of Kenyan Agricultural Development*, London, Overseas Development Institute.

Unakul, S. (1969) "Annual Planning in Thailand," *Economic Bulletin for Asia and the Far East*, 1 (20), 68–80.

United Nations (1961) *A Handbook of Public Administration*, New York, Technical Assistance Bureau, United Nations.

160 DEVELOPMENT PROJECTS AS POLICY EXPERIMENTS

United Nations Development Program (UNDP) (1969) *An Evaluation of UNDP Assistance to Uganda*, New York, United Nations.

UNDP (1972) *UNDP Assistance Requested by the Government of Thailand for the Period 1972–1976*, New York, United Nations.

UNDP (1973) *The UNDP Program in Nigeria: Report of the Evaluation Mission*, New York, United Nations.

UNDP (1973a) *UNDP Assistance Requested by the Government of Mexico for the Period 1973–1977*, New York, United Nations.

UNDP (1973b) "Investment Follow-up Guidelines," mimeographed, New York, United Nations.

UNDP (1974) *UNDP Operational and Financial Manual*, New York, United Nations.

UNDP (1979) *Rural Development: Issues and Approaches for Technical Cooperation*, Evaluation Study No. 2, New York, United Nations.

United Nations Economic Commission for Africa (1969) "Development Planning and Economic Integration in Africa," *Journal of Development Planning* (1), 109–56.

United Nations Economic Commission for Asia and the Far East (1969) "The Planning and Financing of Social Development in the ECAFE Region," *Economic Bulletin for Asia and the Far East*, 1 (20), 4–37.

United States Agency for International Development (USAID) (1970) *Brazil – Education Sector Loan II*, Washington, D.C., USAID.

USAID (1972) *An Evaluation of the Management of Technical Assistance: Projects in Three African Countries*, Washington, D.C., USAID.

USAID (1972a) "Comments on Sector Analysis and Sector Loans in Latin America," unpublished paper, Washington, D.C., USAID.

USAID (1972b) "Sector Lending in Latin America," unpublished paper, Washington, D.C., USAID.

USAID (1973) *Implementation of New Directions in Development Assistance*, Report for the US Congress, House Committee on International Relations, Washington, D.C., Government Printing Office.

USAID (1973a) *Report of Operations Appraisal of East Africa*, Washington, D.C., USAID.

USAID (1979) *Country Development Strategy Statement, FY 1981: Pakistan*, Washington, D.C., USAID.

USAID (1979a) *Country Development Strategy Statement, FY 1981: Sri Lanka*, Washington, D.C., USAID.

USAID (1979b) *Country Development Strategy Statement, FY 1981: Burma*, Washington, D.C., USAID.

United States Code Congressional and Administrative News (1973) (2).

United States General Accounting Office (USGAO) (1979) *U.S.*

Development Assistance to the Sahel − *Progress and Problems*, Report B-159652, Washington, D.C., Government Printing Office.

Uphoff, N. and M. Esman (1974) *Local Organization for Rural Development: An Analysis of the Asian Experience*, Ithaca, N.Y., Cornell University Center for International Studies.

Uphoff, N. and W. Ilchman (1972) "Development in the Perspective of Political Economy," in Uphoff and Ilchman (eds) *The Political Economy of Development*, Berkeley, University of California Press.

Valdepenas, V. (1973) "Philippines" in Y. Hoong (ed.) *Development Planning in Southeast Asia*, Singapore, Regional Institution for Higher Education and Development, 262–6.

Vepa, R. (1977) "Implementation: The Problem of Achieving Results," in D. Rondinelli (ed.) *Planning Development Projects*, Stroudsburg, Pa, Hutchinson & Ross, 169–90.

Villanueva, D. (1971) "A Survey of the Financial System and the Savings-Investment Process in Korea and the Philippines," *Finance and Development* (2), 16–19.

Wade, N. (1974) "Green Revolution: A Just Technology, Often Unjust in Use," *Science*, 186, 1093–6; 1186–8.

Warriner, D. (1964) "Land Reform and Economic Development," in C. Eicher and L. Witt (eds) *Agriculture in Economic Development*, New York, McGraw-Hill, 280–90.

Waterston, A. (1965) *Development Planning: Lessons of Experience*, Baltimore, Md, Johns Hopkins University Press.

Waterston, A. (1971) "An Operational Approach to Development Planning," *International Journal of Health Studies*, 3 (1), 233–52.

Weiss, W., A. Waterston and J. Wilson (1977) "The Design of Agricultural and Rural Development Projects," in D. Rondinelli (ed.) *Planning Development Projects*, Stroudsburg, Pa, Hutchinson & Ross, 95–139.

Wildavsky, A. (1969) "Rescuing Policy Analysis from PPBS," *Public Administration Review*, 2 (29), 189–202.

Wildavsky, A. (1979) *Speaking Truth to Power: The Art and Craft of Policy Analysis*, Boston, Mass., Little, Brown.

World Bank (1967) *Annual Report 1967*, Washington, D.C., World Bank.

World Bank (1974) *Policies and Operations*, Washington, D.C., World Bank.

World Bank (1975) *Rural Development Sector Policy Paper*, Washington, D.C., World Bank.

World Bank (1978) *Annual Review of Project Performance Audit Results*, Washington, D.C., World Bank.

World Bank (1979) *World Development Report 1979*, Washington, D.C., World Bank.

World Bank (1980) *World Development Report 1980*, Washington, D.C., World Bank.

World Bank (1981) *World Development Report 1981*, Washington, D.C., World Bank.

Index

adaptive administration, 89, 112, 116, 130, 148
Adelman, I., 51, 52, 53, 149
adjunctive planning, 140–3
administrative capacity, 34, 40–2, 45, 48, 55, 78, 86, 87, 88, 108, 112, 113, 116, 128, 129, 131, 132, 133, 146
agricultural development, 5, 9, 28, 44, 83, 84, 85, 87, 98, 100, 102, 106, 107, 113, 115
Ahmad, J., 82, 149
Alfonso, F., 15, 153
American Public Health Association, 81, 149
Amin, G., 143, 144, 149
Asher, R., 25, 29, 155

Bainbridge, J., 67, 149
Bangladesh, 51, 93, 96, 98, 110
basic needs, 4, 10, 59, 60, 61, 62
Baum, W., 66, 149
Belshaw, D., 53, 83, 92, 143, 150
beneficiaries, 77–8
Benveniste, G., 6, 17, 149
big-push strategies, 25–7
blueprint approach to project management, 5
Bolivia, 51
Borlaug, N., 97
Botswana, 86
bottlenecks to development, 23, 32–4, 94
bottom-up planning, 30, 31

Brandt Commission, 10, 12, 152
Braybrooke, D., 2, 149
Brazil, 49, 55, 146
Brinkerhoff, D., 126, 159
Bromley, R., 18, 121, 149
Brown, D., 103, 106, 149
budget, 38, 41, 42
Burki, S., 60, 150
Burma, 61, 82
Burns, T., 124, 150
Bustelo, E., 18, 149

Caiden, N., 39, 132, 140, 142, 150
capital, role of in development, 42, 43
Carner, G., 130, 153
Ceylon, see Sri Lanka
Chambers, R., 53, 83, 92, 142, 143, 150
Chang, P., 136, 150
Changrien, P., 31, 41, 150
Cheema, G. S., 133, 135, 150
Chenery, H., 52, 150
Chilalo Agricultural Development Project (CADU), 103
Chile, 51
China, People's Republic of, 12, 60–1, 135, 137, 139
Choldin, H., 93, 98, 150
Clark, W., 13, 18, 153
Cleaves, P., 141, 150
Cohen, J., 99, 103, 144, 150
Cole, D., 36, 150
Colombia, 121, 146
Comilla Project, 93, 96, 98, 102, 110

community development projects, 109, 110
competition, 127
comprehensive planning, see national planning
control-oriented planning, 5–11, 15
coordination, 29, 40, 41, 42, 87, 114, 123, 144
cost-benefit analysis, 3, 16–19, 38, 143, 144
Crane, B., 123, 150
Cuca, R., 92, 97, 99, 100, 102, 150
Currie, L., 26, 151

data, adequacy of, 82–3
Daudzai Project, 94
Davis, J., 6, 151
decentralization, 118–19, 133–6, 145–6
demonstration projects, 20–1, 89, 104–8
development administration theory, 116–20
development policy, 1–5, 7–11, 23–64

economic analysis, 30, 36, 37, 39–40, 69, 72
Ecuador, 84, 87, 113
education, 45–6, 55, 101
employment-generating projects, 60, 102
engaged planning, 132
Enos, J., 32, 43, 151
errors, detection and correction of, 79, 80, 144, 145
Esman, M., 42, 61, 62, 115, 129, 131, 132, 139, 146, 151
Ethiopia, 103
evaluation, 41, 79, 80
Ewing, A., 69, 151
exchange relationships, 114, 123, 124
experimental projects, 19, 20, 90, 91–9
experiments, social, 1, 13–16
experts, 6, 76

family planning projects, 21, 92, 97, 99, 102
Finkle, J., 123, 150
foreign aid, 9, 24, 25, 32, 42, 43, 48, 49, 50, 56, 57, 58
Frankel, F., 108, 151
Friedman, M., 42, 43, 44, 151
Friedmann, J., 131, 151

Ghana, 51
Gittinger, J., 4, 48, 151
goals, 17, 54, 81, 82, 94
Gordenker, L., 86, 122, 151
Grant, J., 57, 151
Griffin, K., 32, 43, 61, 151
Grindle, M., 114, 121, 151
growth-with-equity policy, 4, 9, 50–62
Guatemala, 83, 84
Gurley, J., 137, 152

Hapgood, D., 20, 21, 104, 105, 106, 152
Haque, W., 107, 108, 152
Harbison, F., 45, 46, 152
Harrod–Domar model, 39
health projects, 67, 100
Heginbotham, S., 111, 152
Henderson, P., 12, 152
Hirschman, A., 4, 19, 26, 27, 152
Honduras, 51, 84, 87, 113
Hoos, I., 16, 55, 152
Hoselitz, B., 33, 152
housing projects, 115
human resources development, 45–6, 52, 61, 64
Humphrey, D., 30, 152
Hussain, I., 41, 152
Hutchinson, E., 84, 152

Ilchman, W., 4, 161
incentives, 84–5, 101, 113, 123, 124, 145–7
India, 8, 29, 100, 103, 106, 109, 110, 146, 148
Indonesia, 30, 39

industrialization policies, 8, 23, 25–8, 42
industry, small-scale, 82
innovations, 100, 103, 104, 105, 107, 124, 144–5
institution-building, 45, 128–30
Intensive Agricultural Districts Program (IADP), 103
International Labor Office (ILO), 10, 46, 60, 152

Jackson, R., 50, 153
Japan, 137, 139
Johnston, B., 13, 18, 44, 153
Joint Commission for Rural Reconstruction (JCRR), 126

Karunatilake, H., 37, 38, 41, 153
Katz, S., 116, 153
Kenya, 83, 92, 118, 123, 146
Khan, A., 61, 94, 151, 153
Kilby, P., 80, 82, 86, 87, 153
Kim, J. K., 92, 153
Kim, K., 92, 101, 153
Kim, O., 92, 101, 153
Korea, South, 12, 29, 30, 31, 36, 49, 51, 56, 73, 92, 95, 140
Korten, D., 15, 89, 96, 130, 153
Kulp, E., 106, 153
Kuznets, S., 28, 154

Lamb, G., 127, 154
land development projects, 100, 101, 113, 115, 135
Landau, M., 117, 154
LaPorte, R., 36, 154
leadership, 95, 115
leading sector strategies, 25, 26
learning process, 15, 89, 97, 116, 120, 128–31
Ledesma, A., 137, 154
Lee, E., 61, 154
Lee, H. B., 117, 154
Lee Kuan Yew, 115
Lele, U., 20, 154
Leonard, D., 111, 123, 154

Lewis, A., 26, 154
Lim, D., 37, 39, 154
Lindblom, C., 2, 13, 74, 141, 147, 148, 154
logical framework, 70
Lyman, P., 36, 140

McNamara, R., 9, 10, 64, 154
Maithreyan, B., 140, 155
Majone, G., 14, 155
Malawi, 86, 122
Malaysia, 29, 37, 39, 42, 48, 56, 115
management systems, 3, 48, 74–87
Mangahas, M., 74, 155
market surrogates, 127, 128
Marshall Plan, 24
Marzouk, G., 38, 40, 155
Mason, E., 25, 29, 155
Mauritania, 75
Mellor, J., 44, 153
Meltsner, A., 17, 155
Mexico, 93, 99, 114, 146
Mikesell, R., 25, 155
Montgomery, J., 61, 62, 131, 132, 135, 146, 155
Morawetz, D., 50, 51, 155
Moris, J., 103, 104, 106, 112, 119, 132, 155
Morocco, 86
Morris, C., 51, 52, 149
Morss, E., 5, 98, 100, 155
Mueller, P., 102, 155
Murphy, D., 55, 155
Myrdal, G., 29, 33, 155

national planning, 6, 28–32, 34–44
natural experiments, 96–7
Nelson, M., 101, 113, 155
Nepal, 36, 37, 39, 40, 115
Niehoff, R., 102, 155
Nigam, S., 8, 156
Niger, 75, 76
Nigeria, 73, 81, 102
Nophaket, S., 36, 156
Noranitipadungkarn, C., 76, 156
Nurkse, R., 27, 156

organizational structure, 98, 106, 110, 111, 112, 119, 124–8, 137–40
Onunkwo, E., 73, 156
Ostrander, F., 86, 156

Paine, S., 61, 156
Pakistan, 29, 31, 41, 82
Paolillo, C., 58, 156
Park, Chung-Hee, 101
participation, 77–8, 130, 131, 137
patron–client relationship, 107, 114, 121, 136
Pearson Commission, 7, 8, 49, 50, 156
performance agreements, 128
Peru, 146
Philippines, 8, 29, 35, 36, 38, 73, 81, 96, 114, 130
Pierce, C., 92, 97, 99, 100, 102, 150
pilot projects, 20, 89, 99–104, 109
Poats, R., 97, 156
Point-Four Program, 24
political commitment, 35–9, 54, 99, 103, 109, 115, 118, 123
political interaction, 1, 6, 15, 85, 86, 104, 120–4
poverty, 5, 7, 8, 9, 11, 27, 33, 49, 52, 59–64, 81
Powell, J., 36, 156
preinvestment analysis, 48, 67, 69, 71
production projects, see replication projects
program loans, 47–8
project cycles, 65–74
projects: appraisal of, 48, 66, 72, 77, 144; definition of, 4; design, 5, 19, 46, 47, 65–74, 144; evaluation of, 66, 79, 80; identification process, 4, 37, 66, 67, 69; implementation of, 11–13, 19, 71; monitoring, 41, 79, 80, 107; planning of, 11–13, 65–72; preparation, 4, 46–7, 66, 70
Prybyla, J., 61, 156
Puebla Project, 93, 97
Pye, L., 118, 156
Pyle, D., 99, 109, 156

quantification, problems of, 16, 82, 83, 143, 144
Quick, S., 121, 126, 156

Rahim, S., 102, 110, 157
Rana, P., 36, 37, 39, 40, 157
Razak, Tun Abdul, 115
replication projects, 21, 89, 108–15
revolutions, 141, 142
Riggs, F., 116, 157
Rondinelli, D., 3, 6, 13, 34, 48, 67, 69, 74, 111, 112, 118, 124, 133, 134, 135, 138, 141, 146, 157, 158
Rosenstein-Rodan, P., 27, 158
Rostow, W., 28, 158
Ruddle, K., 34, 112, 138, 158
Rudner, M., 28, 158
rural development, 9, 58, 59, 75, 77, 95, 100, 103, 105, 108, 110, 134, 137, 138
Ruttan, V., 138, 158
Rwanda, 51

Saemaul Undong, 92, 95, 96, 101, 105
Sahel, 75, 76, 78, 79, 87
Sapire, S., 67, 149
Sapolski, H., 16, 55, 158
Schick, A., 16, 55, 158
Schlesinger, J., 18, 158
Schultz, T., 26, 44, 158
Schulz, L., 39, 158
Scott, J., 136, 158
sectoral planning, 44–9, 51, 53
Seers, D., 32, 158
Self, P., 17, 18, 158
Senegal, 75, 76
service delivery projects, 108–15, 137–40
Shaefer-Kehnert, W., 21, 158
Siffin, W., 116, 117, 158
Singapore, 29, 34, 115
small-scale projects, 142
Smith, T., 135, 159
social change, 12, 116, 117, 141
social learning, 1, 11, 128–31

"special publics," 24, 58, 61–2, 132
Special Rural Development Program
  (SRDP), 83, 92, 93, 95, 98, 100
Spengler, J., 117, 159
Sri Lanka (Ceylon), 29, 36, 37, 38,
  41, 61, 82, 96, 115
Stalker, G., 124, 150
Stavis, B., 139, 159
Strachan, H., 77, 159
strategic planning, 140–3
Streeten, P., 33, 60, 159
Subido, C., 74, 155
Sudan, 84, 118, 145, 146
Sussman, G., 109, 110, 159
synoptic analysis, 2, 5–11, 16–18, 55,
  74–88

Taiwan, 12, 29, 49, 51, 56, 135, 137,
  140
Tanzania, 86, 118, 122
"targetting" of aid projects, 58–62
Taylor, K., 69, 159
technical assistance, 50
technocracy, 5–11
technology transfer, 78, 106, 110
Tendler, J., 84, 87, 113, 114, 159
Thailand, 8, 31, 35, 36, 38, 39, 41,
  96
Thimm, H., 84, 159
Thomas, J., 77, 159
Thomas, T., 126, 159
Thomson, V., 129, 159
top-down planning, 30, 31
training, 146, 147
Trapman, C., 111, 159
trickle-down development strategies,
  1, 7, 34, 51, 52, 62
Tunisia, 85, 86

Unakul, S., 35, 38, 39, 40, 41, 159
uncertainty, 10, 12, 14, 17, 76, 80,
  120, 124
United Nations Development
  Programme (UNDP), 67, 70, 77,
  79, 81, 88, 160
United States Agency for
  International Development
  (USAID), 8, 47–8, 55, 59, 69, 70,
  75, 76, 78, 81, 82, 83, 84, 85, 86,
  87, 160
United States aid policy, 9, 24, 29,
  45–8, 56–8
United States Foreign Assistance Act
  of 1973, 9, 56–7
United States General Accounting
  Office (USGAO), 75, 78, 87, 160
Uphoff, N., 3, 139, 161
Upper Volta, 51

Valdepenas, V., 36, 161
Vepa, R., 115, 161
Villanueva, D., 140, 161

Wade, N., 108, 161
Warriner, D., 45, 161
Waterston, A., 4, 29, 46, 47, 108, 161
Weiss, W., 108, 109, 161
Wildavsky, A., 13, 14, 16, 39, 55, 74,
  89, 91, 132, 140, 142, 150, 155,
  161
Wilson, J., 108, 109, 161
World Bank, 3, 7, 11, 19, 24, 29, 47,
  58, 59, 61, 63, 66, 71, 72, 73, 83,
  85, 122, 123, 133, 161

Zambia, 76, 121, 122, 146
Zevering, K., 102, 155